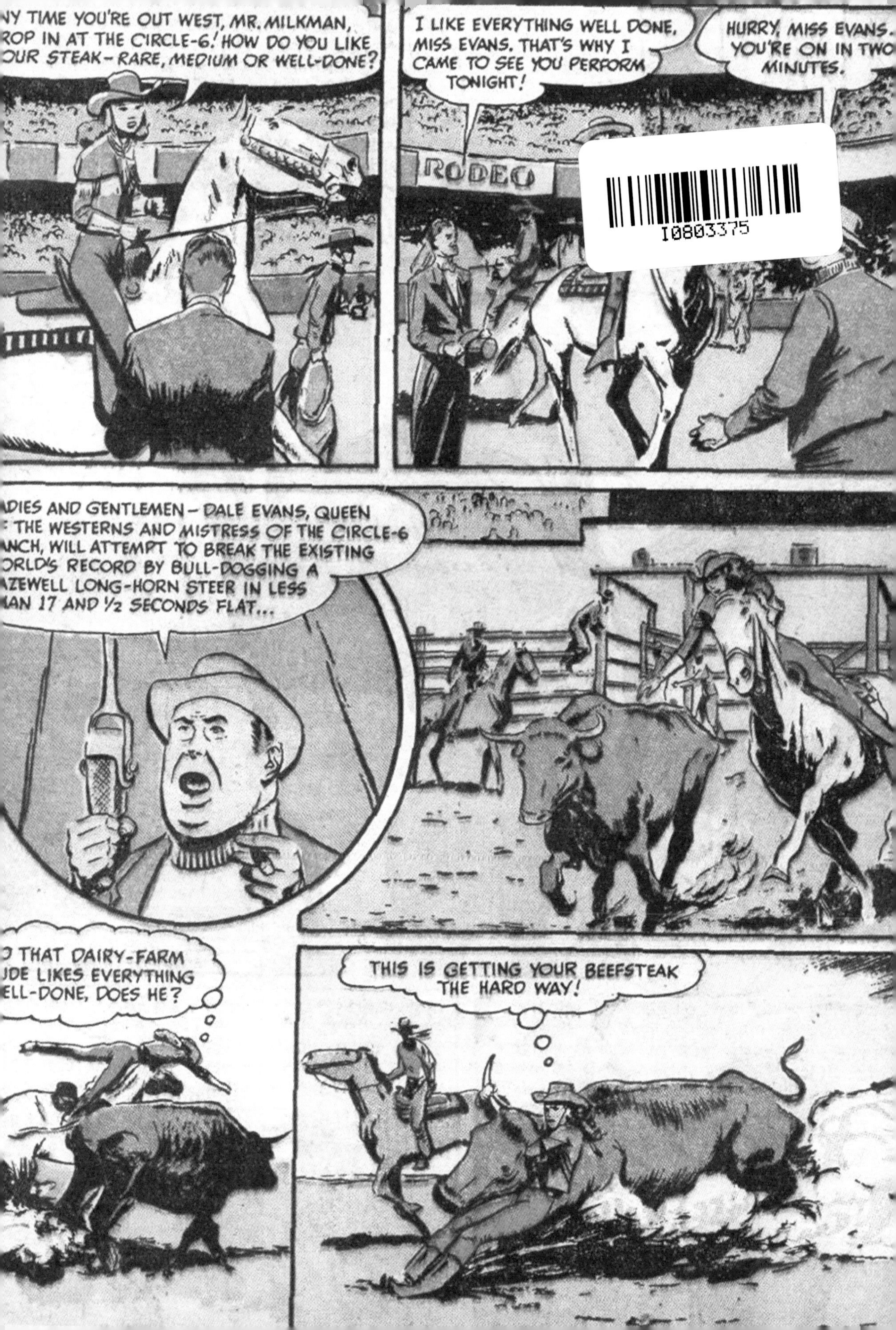
NY TIME YOU'RE OUT WEST, MR. MILKMAN, ROP IN AT THE CIRCLE-6! HOW DO YOU LIKE OUR STEAK - RARE, MEDIUM OR WELL-DONE?
I LIKE EVERYTHING WELL DONE, MISS EVANS. THAT'S WHY I CAME TO SEE YOU PERFORM TONIGHT!
HURRY, MISS EVANS. YOU'RE ON IN TWO MINUTES.
RODEO
ADIES AND GENTLEMEN - DALE EVANS, QUEEN THE WESTERNS AND MISTRESS OF THE CIRCLE-6 ANCH, WILL ATTEMPT TO BREAK THE EXISTING ORLD'S RECORD BY BULL-DOGGING A AZEWELL LONG-HORN STEER IN LESS HAN 17 AND 1/2 SECONDS FLAT...
O THAT DAIRY-FARM UDE LIKES EVERYTHING ELL-DONE, DOES HE?
THIS IS GETTING YOUR BEEFSTEAK THE HARD WAY!

Nancy Davidson

COWGIRL

Cofounders: Taj Forer and Michael Itkoff

Designer: Ursula Damm

Copy editor: Laura Fredrickson

ISBN 978-0-9897981-9-8

Printed in China

Daylight Books

E-mail: info@daylightbooks.org

Web: www.daylightbooks.org

Table of Contents

COWGIRL

WORK

NANCY DAVIDSON

Why the Rodeo Cowgirl

Nancy Davidson is an interdisciplinary artist, working primarily in sculpture and installation. Davidson grew up in Chicago and received a BFA from the University of Illinois at Chicago. In 1975, she received her MFA from the School of the Art Institute of Chicago, where she began her professional career, exhibiting in solo and group shows in 1977 and 1978, including at the Museum of Contemporary Art Chicago, the Art Institute of Chicago, and the Walker Art Center in Minneapolis. Creative Capital funded Davidson's Cowgirl *research and project. The resulting show,* Dustup, *exhibited at the Betty Cuningham Gallery, New York, in the fall of 2012, and an expanded version exhibited at the Boca Raton Museum of Art in Boca Raton, Florida, in 2013. In addition to a Guggenheim fellowship, Davidson's honors include grants from the National Endowment for the Arts (1979); Yaddo residencies (1980, 2003); the Anonymous Was a Woman Award (1997); and grants from the Pollock-Krasner Foundation (2001) and Creative Capital (2005). Davidson's work has been reviewed in the* New York Times, Art in America, Artforum, *the* Village Voice, *the* Brooklyn Rail, Der Spiegel, *and* Art & Text.

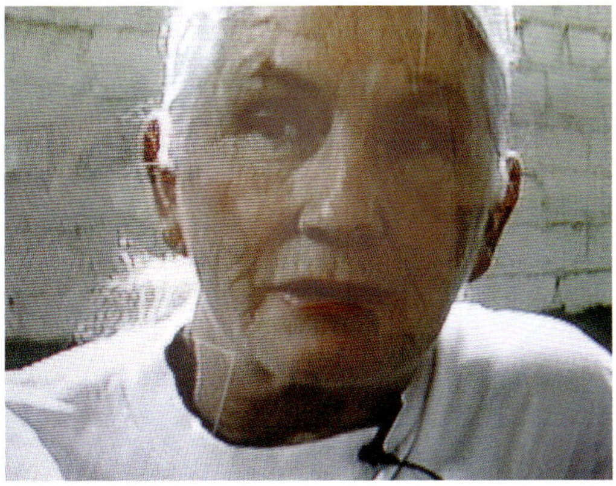

Jan Youren,
video still, 1993

by Nancy Davidson

In 2005, I was in Fort Worth, Texas, doing research at the National Cowgirl Museum and Hall of Fame. A Women's Professional Rodeo event was taking place in the ring next to the museum. Never having attended a rodeo, I didn't know what to expect, so I went. I captured on video the last bucking bronco ride of rodeo champion Jan Youren's 47-year career. She rodeoed until the age of 63, when she retired with five world championships in bareback bronc riding, 13 reserve championships in bareback, and 15 reserve championships in bull riding. I couldn't believe someone who was 63 would be riding in such a physically hair-raising way. Rodeo became an obsession for me. I had to find out who these cowgirls were and what their history was. Rodeo cowgirls did things that were unacceptable. Youren was an American icon. All the ideas about popular tropes and stereotypes I had previously worked with were imbedded in the rodeo cowgirl.

Even as a child in the '50s, I was inspired by the cowgirl character and her can-do spirit—rhinestone cowgirls in Hollywood films and musicals, such as Doris Day as Calamity Jane. My memories set off an exploration into the history and legend of cowgirls and the American West. The embodiment of a free-spirited woman with agency appeared as a guide. What began as a childhood attraction to the cowgirl became a reinvention celebrating and critiquing popular culture.

COW

GIRL

IN MY COWGIRL BOOTS

Leisl Carr Childers is an assistant professor of history and the coordinator of the public history program at the University of Northern Iowa. During her doctoral work at the University of Nevada, Las Vegas, she pursued an interest in cowboy culture and rodeo sport as a curatorial fellow at the Autry National Center of the American West. While in residence at the Autry, she curated an exhibition on Gene Autry's Flying A Rodeo for the Museum of the American West's Founder's Day, which traveled to the National Finals Rodeo in December 2008 for the event's 50th anniversary. Her article on the National Finals Rodeo and its place in the urban environment also appeared in that winter's Nevada Historical Society Quarterly. *Her current book with the University of Oklahoma Press,* The Size of the Risk: A History of Multiple Use in the 20th-Century Great Basin, *is an outgrowth of her work on the award-winning Nevada Test Site Oral History Project.*

by Leisl Carr Childers

My first western boots were a tan pair of Acmes with cockroach-killer pointed toes, tall machine-stitched shafts, and wedged heels that made a nice hard sound on my parents' wood floors. They were cheap, but they were important because they gave me that first sense of identity, that I was a cowgirl. To be truthful, I was the furthest thing from a real cowgirl; I grew up in the suburbs of Los Angeles and Salt Lake City before I moved to the classically Western town of Prescott, Arizona. I wanted nothing more than to learn to ride horses well enough to rodeo. Luckily for me, I had friends sympathetic to my ambitions who occasionally invited me out to ride with them in the vast empty spaces that used to be the grasslands surrounding the rocky valley where Prescott is sited.

I rode in those Acme boots for years. From Prescott, I took them to college in California, where I found work-study employment in the school's stables, mucking stalls and exercising horses so that the students taking the university's riding classes could mount up on "calm" horses. Those boots stood me in good stead when I bought my first horse, a seven-year-old mustang pulled off the range near Ridgecrest, California, at two years old. He was an ornery animal that had thrown better riders than me, but every time I pulled my boots on to go saddle him up, I pulled on the confidence of experience.

From Acme, I graduated to a string of nondescript, machine-made boots that I barely remember. Some were tan and classic, some black and buckaroo; I even had a pair of lace-up packers that nearly cost me a broken ankle when I failed to remove my left foot from the stirrup on a dismount. One pair I left in Germany with a young woman near Eppstein in the Taunus Mountains who wanted to be a cowgirl, too. She taught me how to jump her Haflinger over 12-inch obstacles, and I taught her to ride bareback the little one-eyed Arabian I had leased. The value of a good pair of boots did not really sink in until I met a trio of rodeo women—Ann, Jami, and Jordan Bassett—back in Arizona. They bought me my first pair of serious cowgirl boots—the kind meant for riding barrels and roping—after mocking my greenhorn knowledge of proper footwear.

The Bassetts are a multigenerational rodeo clan. John has trained horses his entire life, as his father, Joe, did a generation before him and as his son Joe does today. Ann was a Prescott Frontier Days Rodeo Queen finalist in the 1970s and had tried riding rough stock in rodeos during her youth. In 2003, she won the National Senior Pro Rodeo Association Finals Championship in barrel racing on Paint, a horse I can only dream of riding. Her daughters, Jami and Jordan, grew up on the Arizona

Junior Rodeo and Arizona High School Rodeo Association circuits doing goat tying, team roping, and barrel racing. Today, these cowgirls train their own horses, such as Jimbo, Foxx, Cocomo Jo, Shadow, and a host of others whose names I have yet to learn. The entire family across three generations has more prize saddles and buckles than any other I have ever met, and the cowgirls won most of them.

Every time Ann, Jami, and Jordan pull on their boots—their Justins, Dan Posts, Ariats, and Corrals—they pull on decades' worth of experience in the saddle. Every time they rubber-band their low-heeled ropers to the stirrups, they invoke all the grit and competitiveness of every cowgirl who has gone before them. They scoffed at my pointed-toe, wedge-heeled boots and declared them uncomfortable and unsafe for rodeoing and riding in general. Instead, they bought me a pair of boots that would not get me injured, and they laughed at my naïveté when I asked about the difference.

Not all cowgirl boots are working boots, however, and the Bassetts and I share a fascination with the expensive, handcrafted boots made by the likes of Lucchese, Paul Bond, and Rocketbuster. The class of cowgirl who dons these boots—at several thousand dollars a pair—may never rodeo, and she certainly would not compete in the dirt wearing them.

Nevertheless, film and television cowgirls such as Dale Evans, Gail Davis, and Reno Browne, who owned several pairs of fancy boots, were accomplished cowgirls in their own right—though their horses Buttermilk, Target, and Major never enjoyed the attention given to their male counterparts' Trigger, Champion, and Lucky. I certainly wanted a pair just like Dale Evans's white silver-studded star boots.

These cowgirls did not always play the sidekick to their cowboy peers Roy Rogers, Gene Autry, and Jimmy Wakely. All three women had comic book series dedicated to chronicling their exploits to avid fans who wanted to be cowgirls, too. Every time they pulled on their white, brown, or black boots and saddled up to shoot a scene, they pulled on years of experience performing on horseback. Historians have chronicled the exploits of the cowgirls these screen legends emulated, such as Prairie Rose Henderson, Mabel Strickland, Lucille Mulhall, and Bonnie McCarroll. The boots those early rodeo cowgirls wore took a beating in the arena, and every time they pulled theirs on, they set the standard for toughness and athleticism for the next century.

I still have those buff-colored, rubber-soled, rounded-toe Ariats that the Bassetts bought for me. Sure, I still am not really a cowgirl, but every time I pull those boots on, I pull on all the years of riding horses I have managed to accumulate and the confidence that comes with even that meager amount of experience. I also have a pair of Enid Justin's Nocona boots, purchased precisely because they bear the stamp of a woman boot maker whose sassy attitude in early 20th-century Texas led her to build her own brand. Someday, perhaps, I will have a pair of Rocketbuster boots, if I am lucky. All that really matters, however, is that the Bassett trio, the Hollywood cowgirls, the early rodeo gals, and I can ride in our cowgirl boots.

COWGIRLS; NEW WOMEN OF THE WEST

Renée M. Laegreid, PhD, is an associate professor of history at the University of Wyoming. Her area of specialty is women and gender in the 20th-century American West, and her publications include Riding Pretty: Rodeo Royalty in the American West *(2006), an exploration of the emergence and development of the rodeo queen phenomenon from 1909 to 1969, and a coedited volume of essays,* Women on the North American Plains *(2011), which provides an overview of the diversity of women and their experiences in this region. She has published numerous essays on women and the rodeo, and she is currently working on a book-length project that examines the media's role in shaping the contemporary image of the cowgirl. Laegreid is also series editor for Women, Gender, and the West, a book series published by Texas Tech University Press.*

by Renée M. Laegreid

Beautiful and daring, feminine yet strong: cowgirls have held a celebrated place in American culture ever since they burst onto the rodeo scene in the 1890s. Women rode horses and worked cattle on family ranches before they appeared in rodeos, of course, but they were not called cowgirls. This moniker first emerged when women began participating in organized rodeos. In the 1890s, the private competitions cowboys had enjoyed during ranch roundups developed into the public sport familiar today. In this new, mass-spectator event, women not only participated, but they also enjoyed celebrity status for their skill and daring.

When, exactly, the word *cowgirl* entered common usage is hard to trace, although Will Rogers is credited with using the term in 1899. Visiting St. Louis that year, Rogers saw little 14-year-old Lucille Mulhall appear in her first public riding and roping contest. Rogers considered her performance there to be the "direct start of what has since come to be known as the Cowgirl.... [T]here was no such a word up to then as Cowgirl."[1] A few years later, President Theodore Roosevelt saw Mulhall perform at a roping exhibition in Oklahoma City. When he referred to her as a cowgirl, reporters covering the president quoted him, newspapers published his comments, and *cowgirl* sprang full force into the American vernacular.[2] Americans across the country became introduced to the term through women's performances in rodeo events based on work associated with cowboys and their ranching chores

At the turn of the last century, Lucille Mulhall enjoyed the title "first American cowgirl." She had the good fortune of being born in an era when her ability to outrope, outshoot, and outride the cowboys on her father's ranch could be parlayed into career options in rodeo and Wild West shows.[3] While the emergence of mass-spectator events provided a venue for her talents, coinciding shifts in social and cultural attitudes made it possible for her to pursue those options. Between 1880 and 1929, the topic of women and their role in society became part of a national debate. Modernists, who advocated gender reform, challenged the Victorian-era limitations on activities considered proper for women. Their efforts succeeded in opening the door for adventurous "new women" like Mulhall to embark on careers outside the home.

Modernists encouraged young, middle-class women to move outside the domestic sphere, to seek out social, economic, and professional opportunities that had been closed to them solely on the basis of their sex. Traditionalists, on the other hand, argued the necessity of women to adhere to the virtues of so-called true womanhood—piety, purity, submission, and domesticity.[4] They stressed the importance of women staying within the confines of their homes in order to focus on family and domestic responsibilities. What would happen to society, they asked, if women should leave their protected sphere and enter the nasty, competitive world of work and politics? The debate over the role of women created controversy aplenty on its own, but combined with the popularity of Sigmund Freud's recently published work that acknowledged women's sexuality (and the birth control movement, which made expressing sexuality easier and safer), civilization itself seemed to hinge on whether or not women maintained gender separation, domestic roles, and passive behaviors.[5]

Rodeo cowgirls emerged during this era of the new woman, and the women who chose to carve out a career on the rodeo circuit found themselves in the middle of the controversy. Ranch wives and daughters who used their skills at home stayed out of the fray; even young ranch women who competed in their local rodeos distanced themselves from professional cowgirls. Ella Granger, reared on a ranch outside of Pendleton, Oregon, competed in the Pendleton Round-Up during the early 1900s. She recalled that the professional cowgirls "would play cards and maybe drink and associated with men all the way around more so than we did.... [W]e didn't know that kind of life." When asked if the cowgirl athletes were "proper women," Granger whispered, "I don't think so."[6] Women who opted to become cowgirls, who "self-consciously crossed boundaries of traditional behavior to express sexuality, individualism, and self-development," became part of the national concern about women. To traditionalists, these new women of the West seemed to have abandoned the obligations of their sex to uphold morality and to become wives and mothers.[7]

Cowgirls participating in arguably the most masculine of sports had to overcome cultural biases in order to gain a favorable public image. One of these biases centered on the association of public performance and immorality; women who took to the stage or any other form of public performance suffered especially tawdry reputations. Another bias concerned a fear that if women participated in masculine activities, they would lose their feminine attributes and become "mannish."[8] Cowgirls countered these biases with purposely feminine behavior and costumes, and by emphasizing their dedication to family life. With sweet smiles, stylishly coiffed hair, and deftly applied powder and lipstick, rodeo cowgirls appeared the epitome of femininity while riding broncs or roping calves. Their costumes, although inspired by practical cowboy attire, "produced new concepts of what it meant to be feminine." The cowgirls adorned their skirts with colorful embroidery, and they wore silk blouses, colorful scarves, and exquisitely tooled boots.[9]

Mabel Strickland exemplifies the new woman of the West in her ability to balance modernist and traditionalist expectations. Petite, beautiful, and a skilled performer, Strickland told a reporter, "You think I'm a paradox. But I belong in the saddle, for I've been there since I was three.... Still, I love dresses and everything that goes with them. I can't tolerate the mannish woman any more than I can stand the womanish man."[10] Even Fox Hastings, who got down and very dirty in the arena while bulldogging steers, insisted she was still very much a woman. When the rodeo ended, she assured reporters, she enjoyed cooking for her husband and loved to sew and make beautifully smocked dresses for her nieces.[11] To counter the notion that rodeo women were immoral and mannish, the cowgirl athletes emphasized their dedication to the traditional values of home, family, and femininity.

Beginning in the mid-1920s, the modernist trends that had encouraged cowgirls to take up rodeo as a professional career began to fade; the golden era of the cowgirl ended just as the Great Depression began. Not until after the Second World War did the image of cowgirls reappear in popular media. But the cowgirl image of the 1950s differed significantly from its predecessor. The direct connection between ranch skills and rodeo performance had been undone, allowing the balance between feminine women performing masculine skills to shift. Popular images of cowgirls, from pinup posters to advertisements, only alluded to—rather than demonstrated—ranch and riding skills, and the earlier emphasis on femininity reappeared as overt sexuality. Loosed from rodeo and ranch moorings, any woman could call herself a cowgirl by donning a pair of boots and a hat and adopting a bit of attitude. Even in the 1960s, when the women's movement fought against sexual stereotyping and women began to enter professional rodeo once again, the connection between strength and sexuality remained a foundation of cowgirl identity.

The definition of cowgirl has broadened since its 19th-century rodeo origins: ranch women identify with the image, but so do singer-songwriters, artists, librarians, women who make their home in the West—or East or South and even North. And why not? The characteristics of the first new women of the West are still evocative and powerful, embracing strength, self-reliance, competency, and femininity. These are the characteristics that first captivated the American public, and they continue to give cowgirls—inside or outside of the rodeo arena—larger-than-life status.

NOTES

1. John Brand, "Lucy Mulhall—The Fist [*sic*] American Cowgirl!," *Buckaroo Leather Horse Tack, Use, Care and Maintenance*, http://buckarooleather.blogspot.com/2011/01/lucille-mulhall-fist-american-cowgirl.html.
2. Michael Bales and Ann Terry Hill, *Pendleton Round-Up* at 100 (Graphic Arts Books, 2009).
3. Beth Day, *America's First Cowgirl* (Julian Messner, 1955).
4. Barbara Welter, "The Cult of True Womanhood: 1820–1860," *American Quarterly* 18, no. 2, Part 1 (Summer 1966).
5. Robert W. Rydell and Rob Kroes, *Buffalo Bill in Bologna* (University of Chicago Press, 2005).
6. Renée M. Laegreid, *Riding Pretty* (University of Nebraska Press, 2006).
7. Paula S. Fass, *The Damned and the Beautiful* (Oxford University Press, 1977).
8. Angela J. Latham, *Posing a Threat* (Wesleyan University Press, 2000).
9. Sarah A. Gordon, "Any Desired Length: Negotiating Gender through Sports Clothing," *Beauty and Business*, ed. Philip Scranton (Routledge, 2001).
10. "Prowess of Girls Shown in He-Man Sport of Rodeo," *Pendleton East Oregonian*, souvenir edition, September 17, 1925.
11. Mary Lou LeCompte, *Cowgirls of the Rodeo* (University of Illinois Press, 1993).

WO

RK

ROWDYANN (2012), pp 21–23

108″ x 74″ x 72″
fabric, foam, wood, plastic, metal

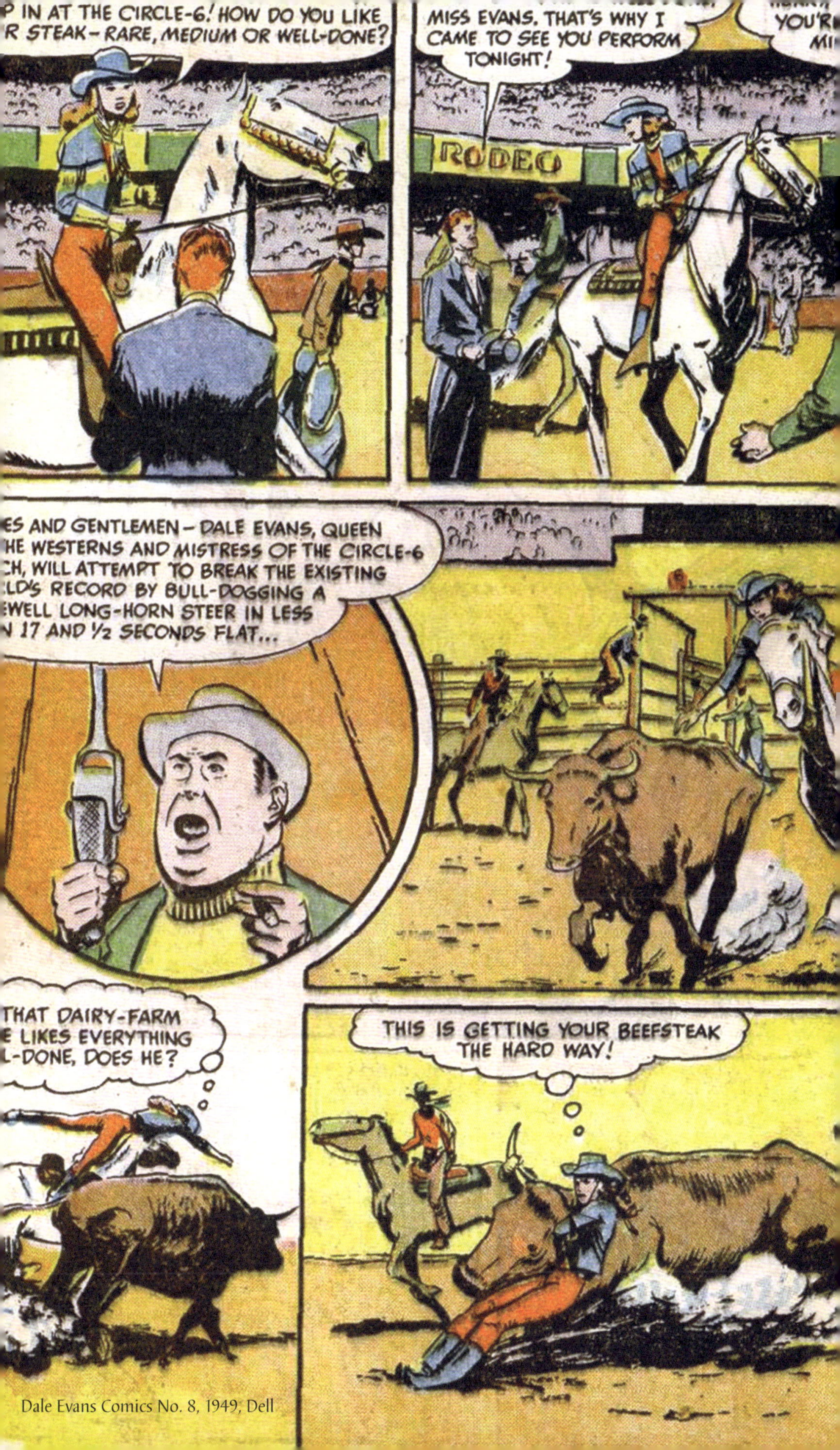

Dale Evans Comics No. 8, 1949, Dell

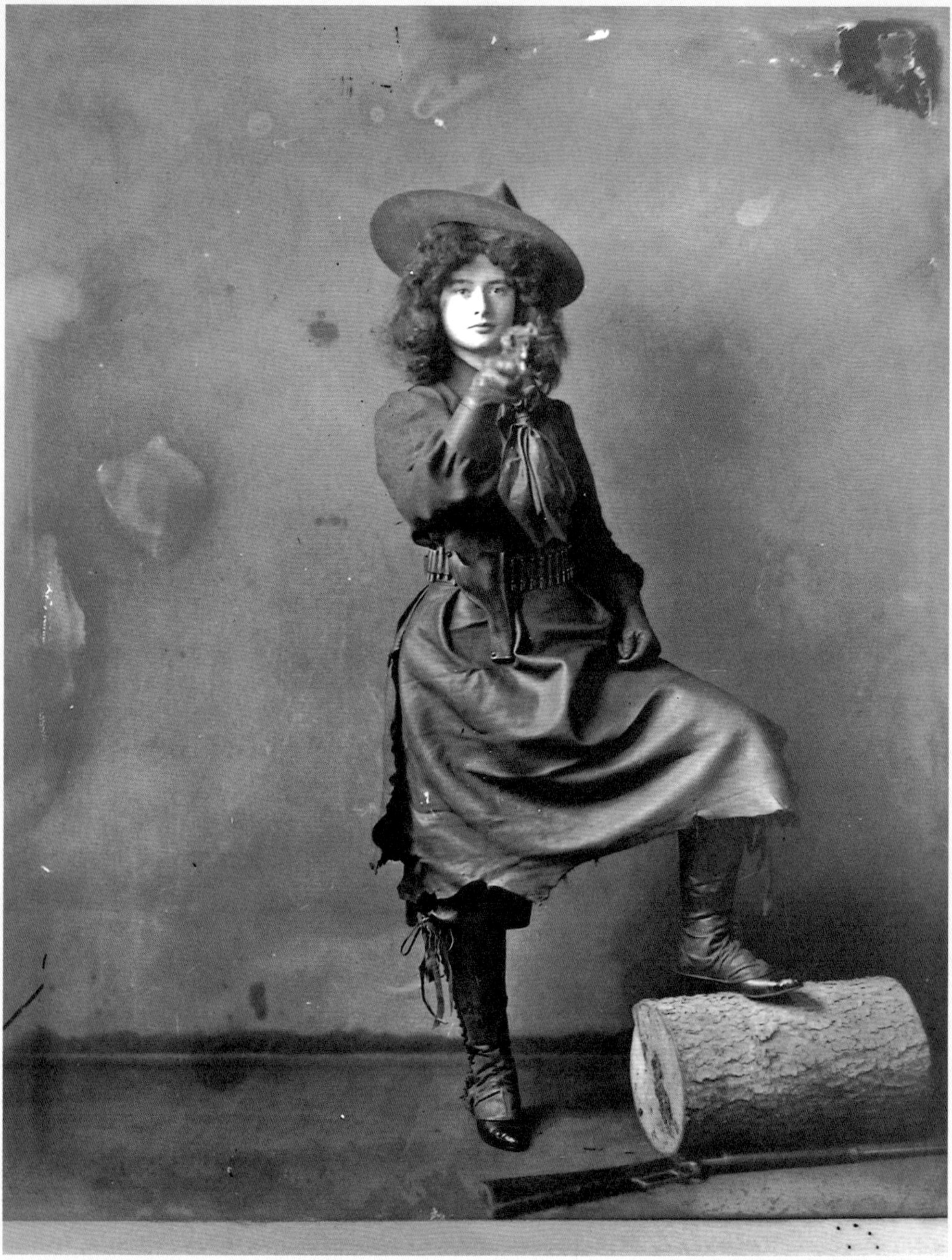

Cowgirl portrait, circa 1910, The Dawson City Museum, Yukon Territory

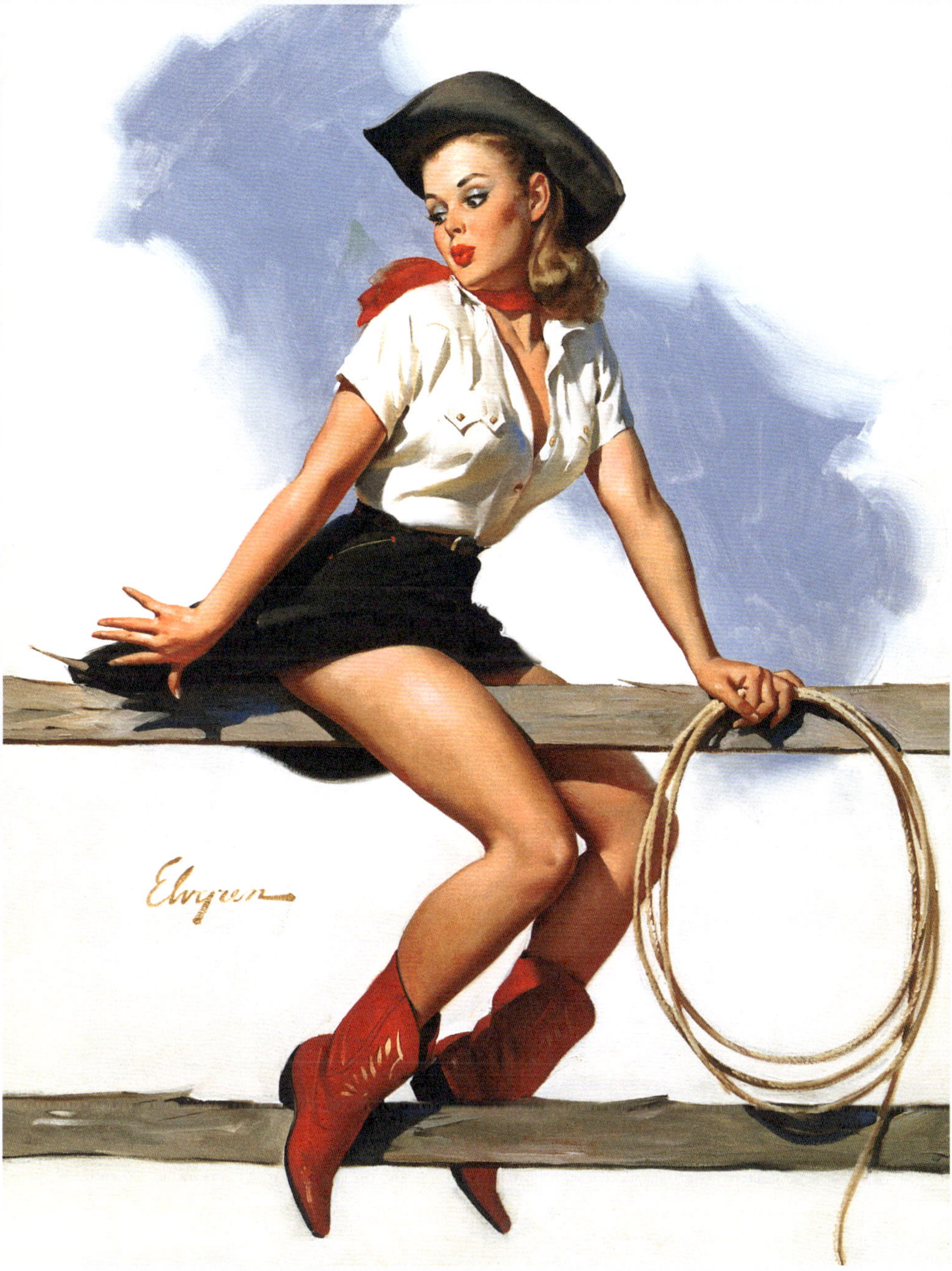

Hi-Ho Silver, Gil Elvgren, 1969 © Brown & Bigelow Inc., St. Paul, Minnesota

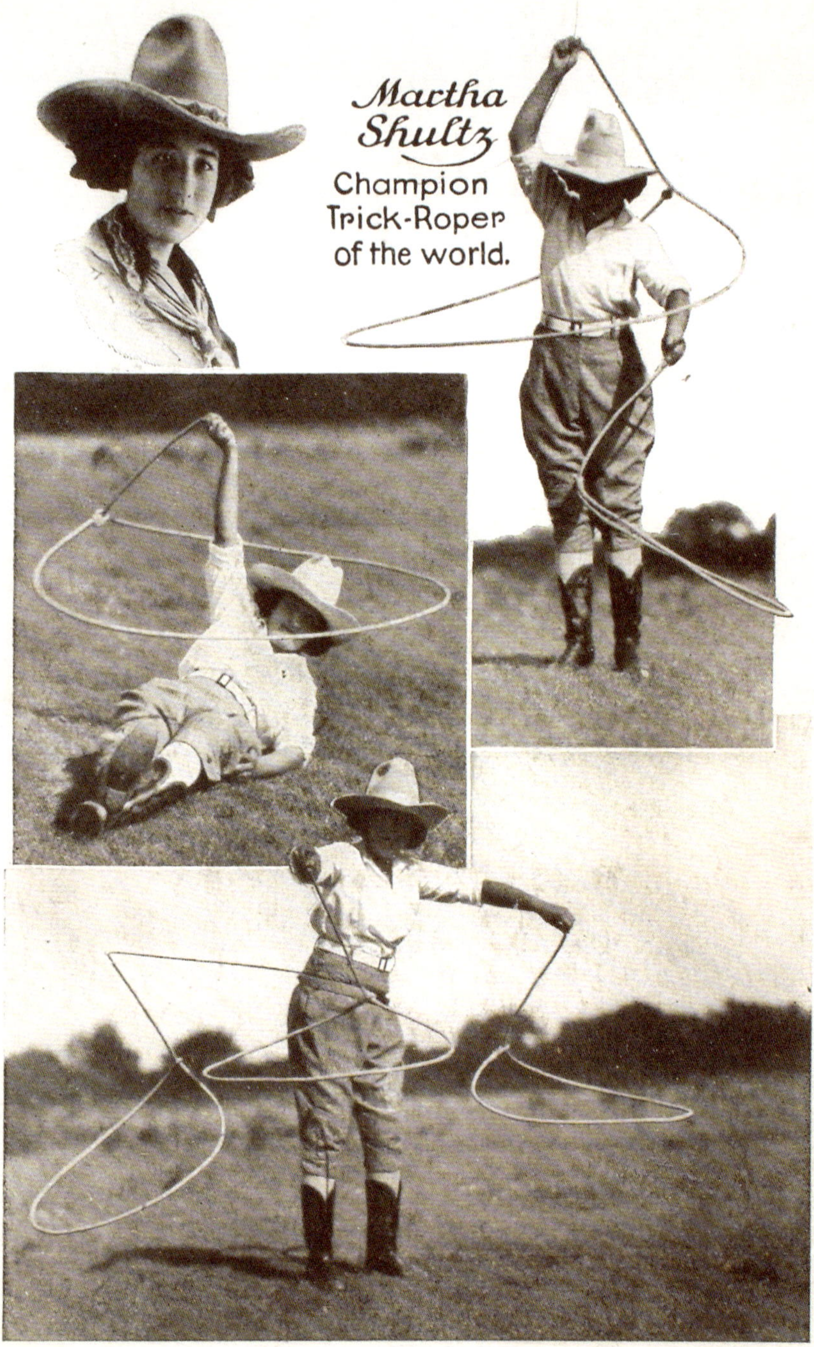

Martha Shultz, champion trick-roper of the world, 1907–1929, Autry National Center

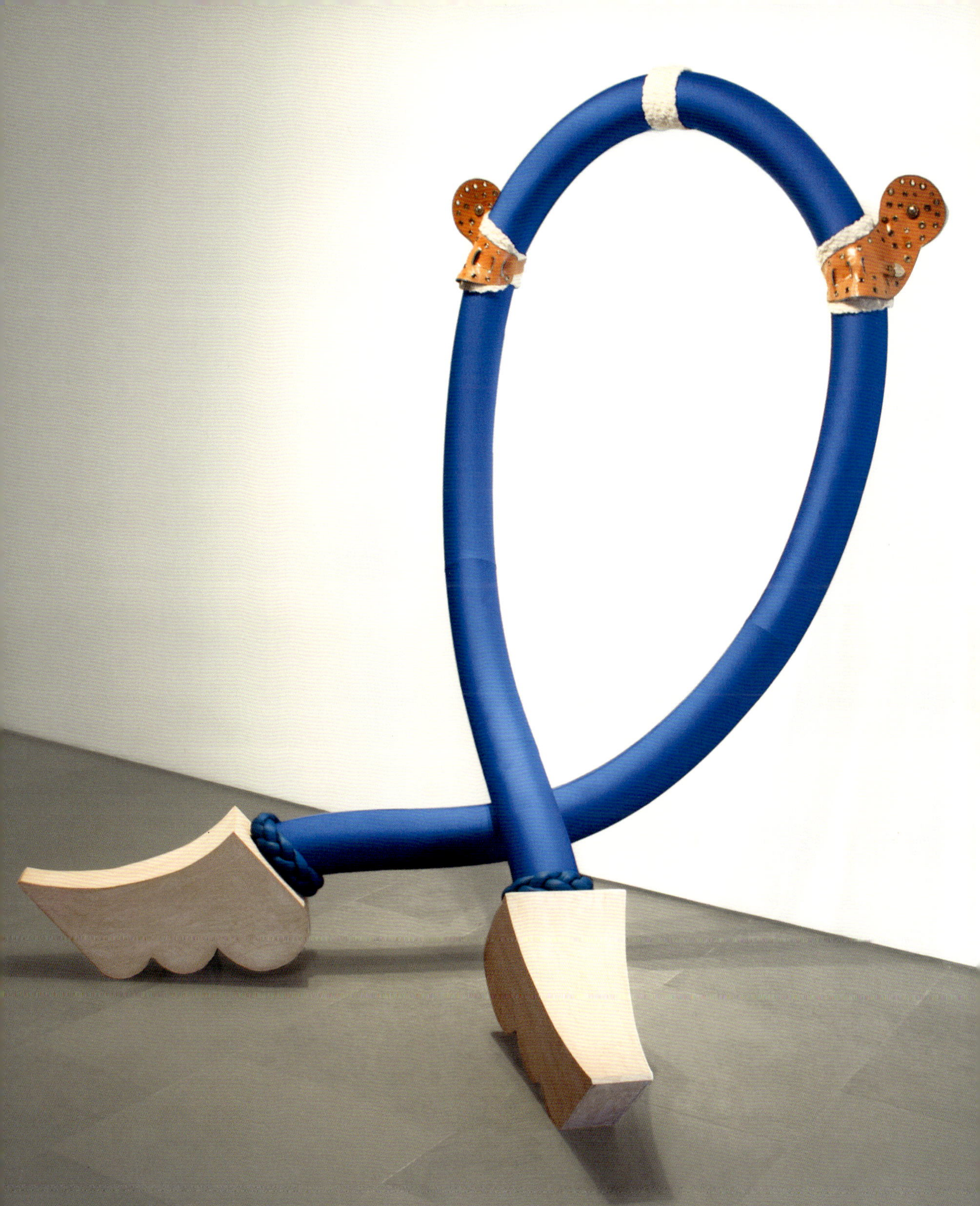

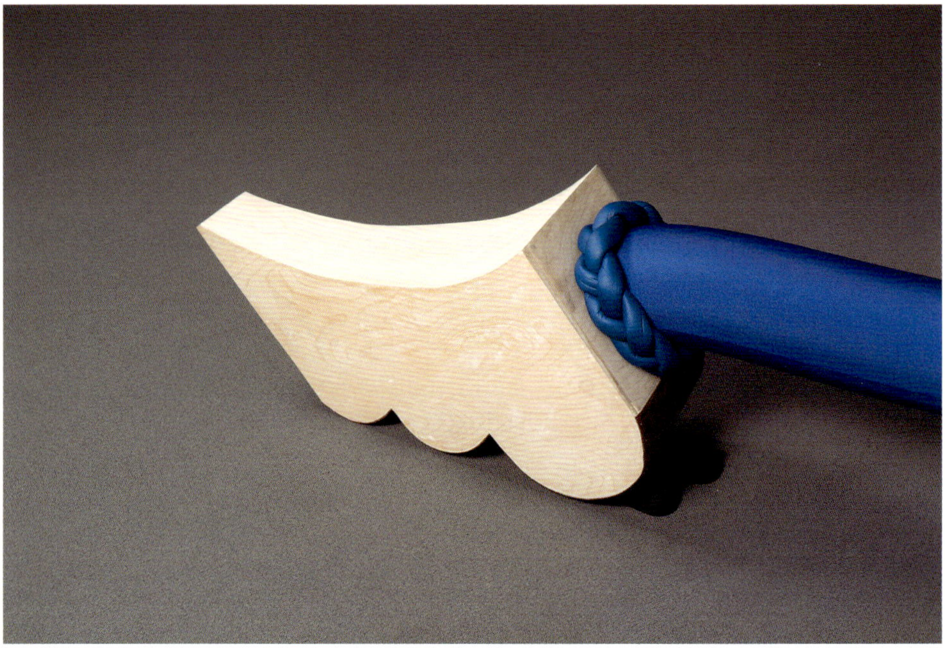

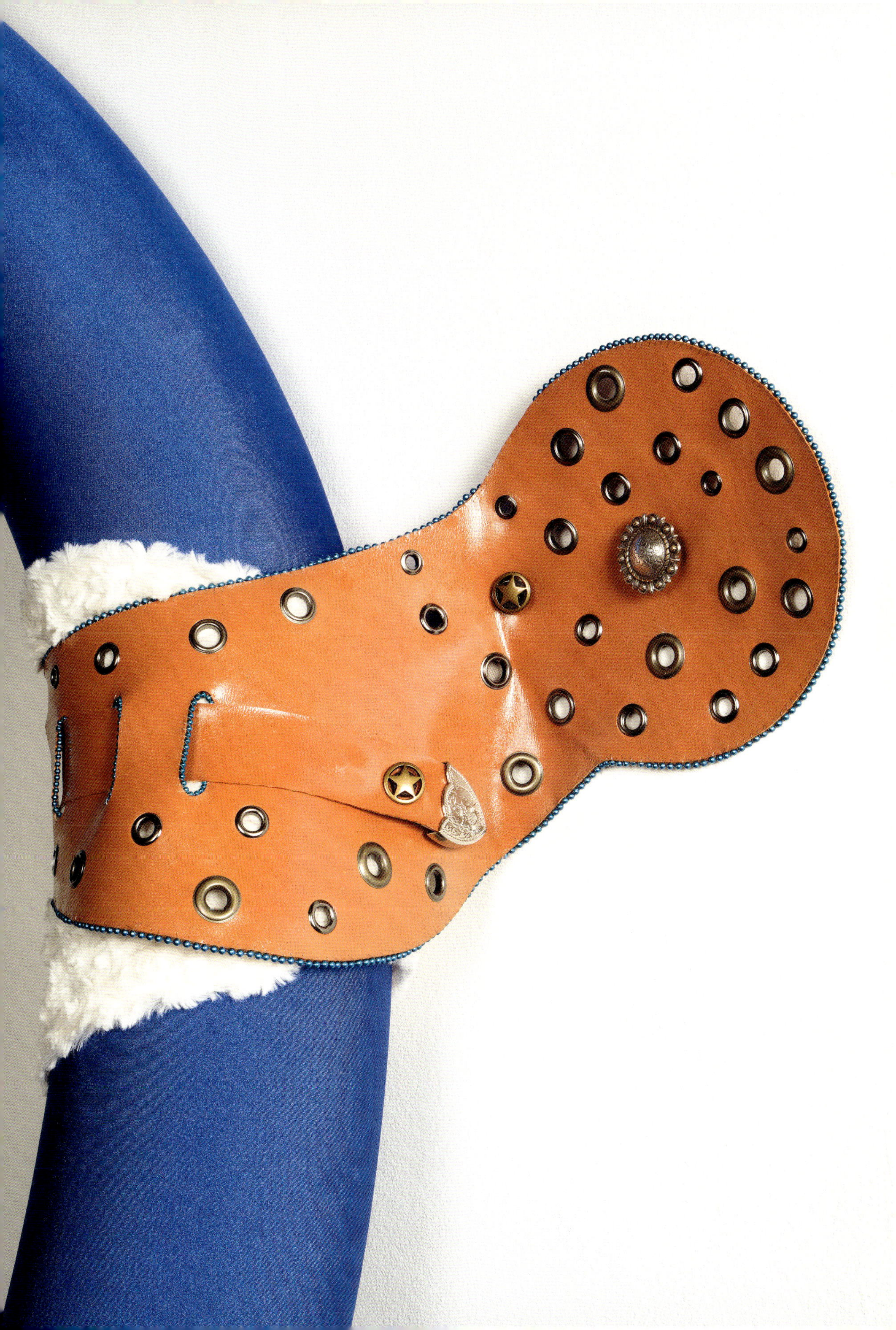

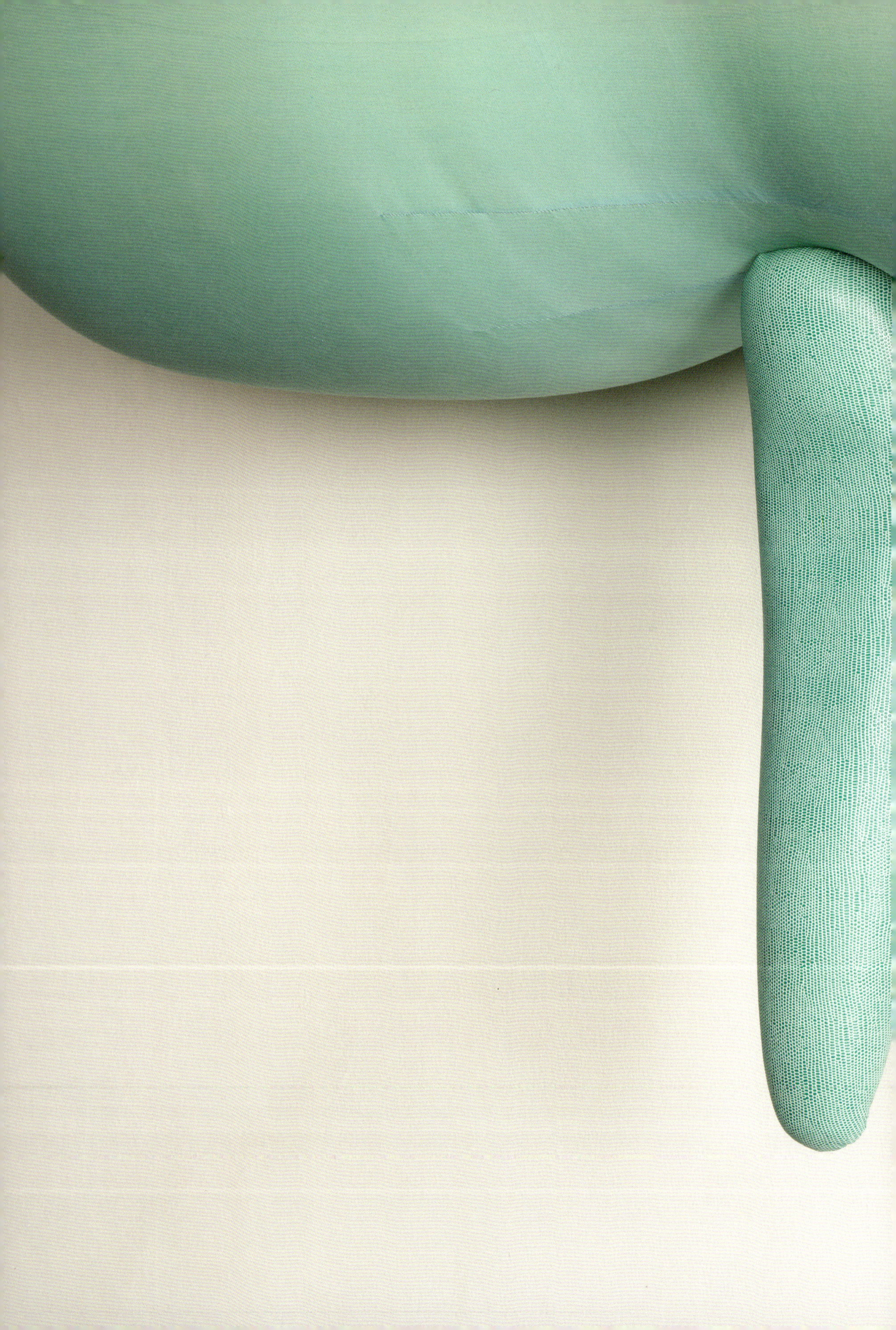

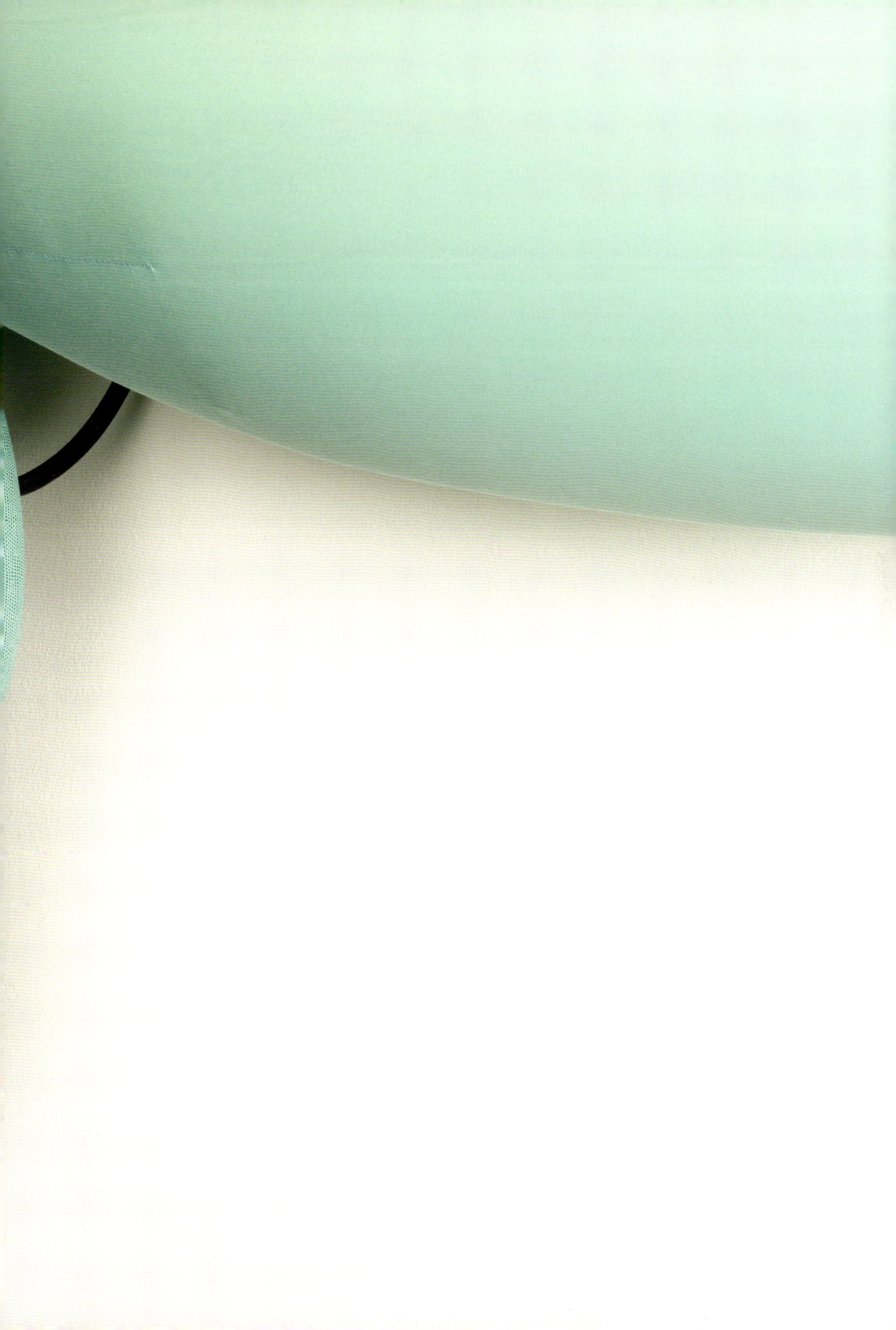

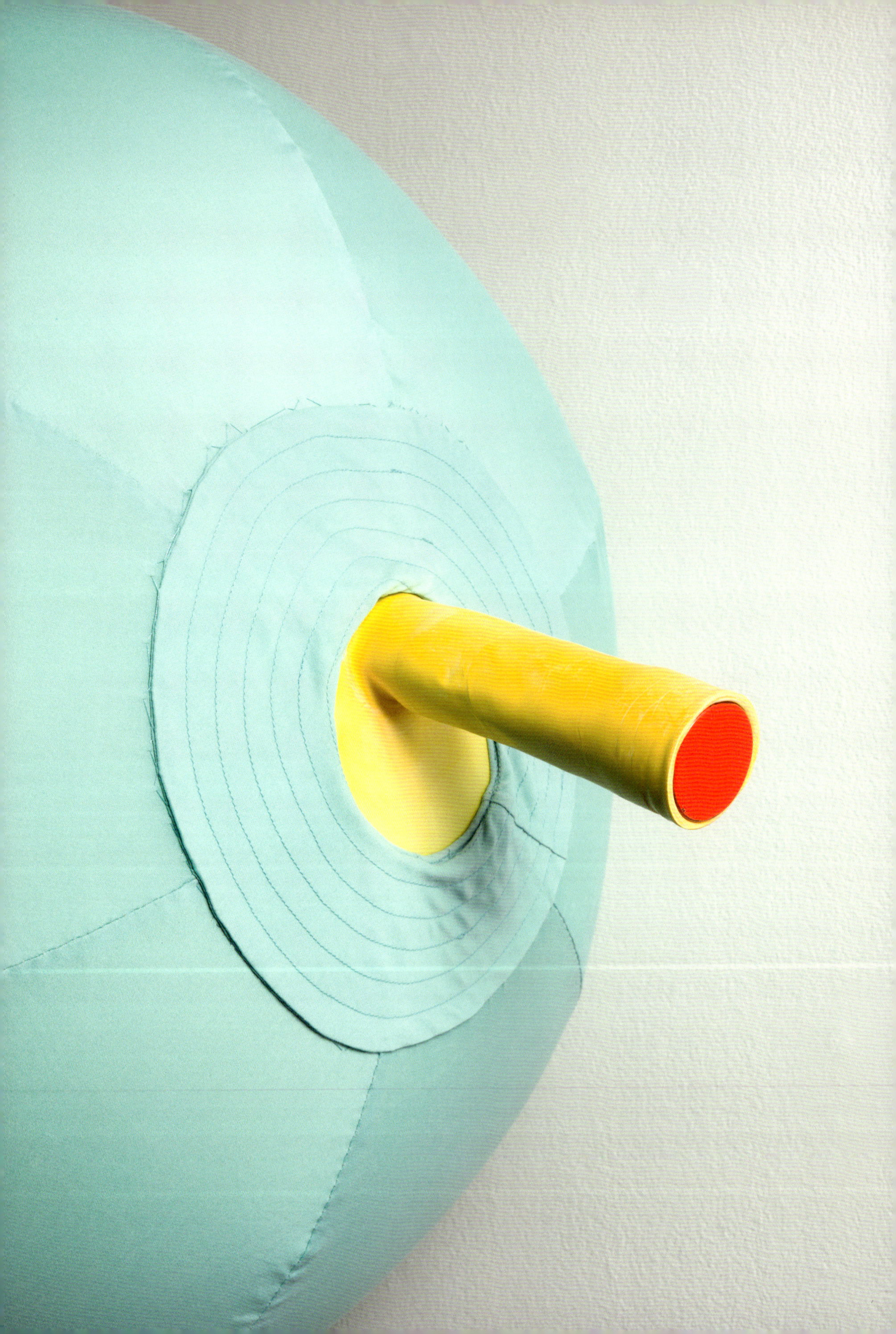

DUDETTE (2007), pp 24–27
43″ x 24″ x 60″
latex, fabric, plastic, metal

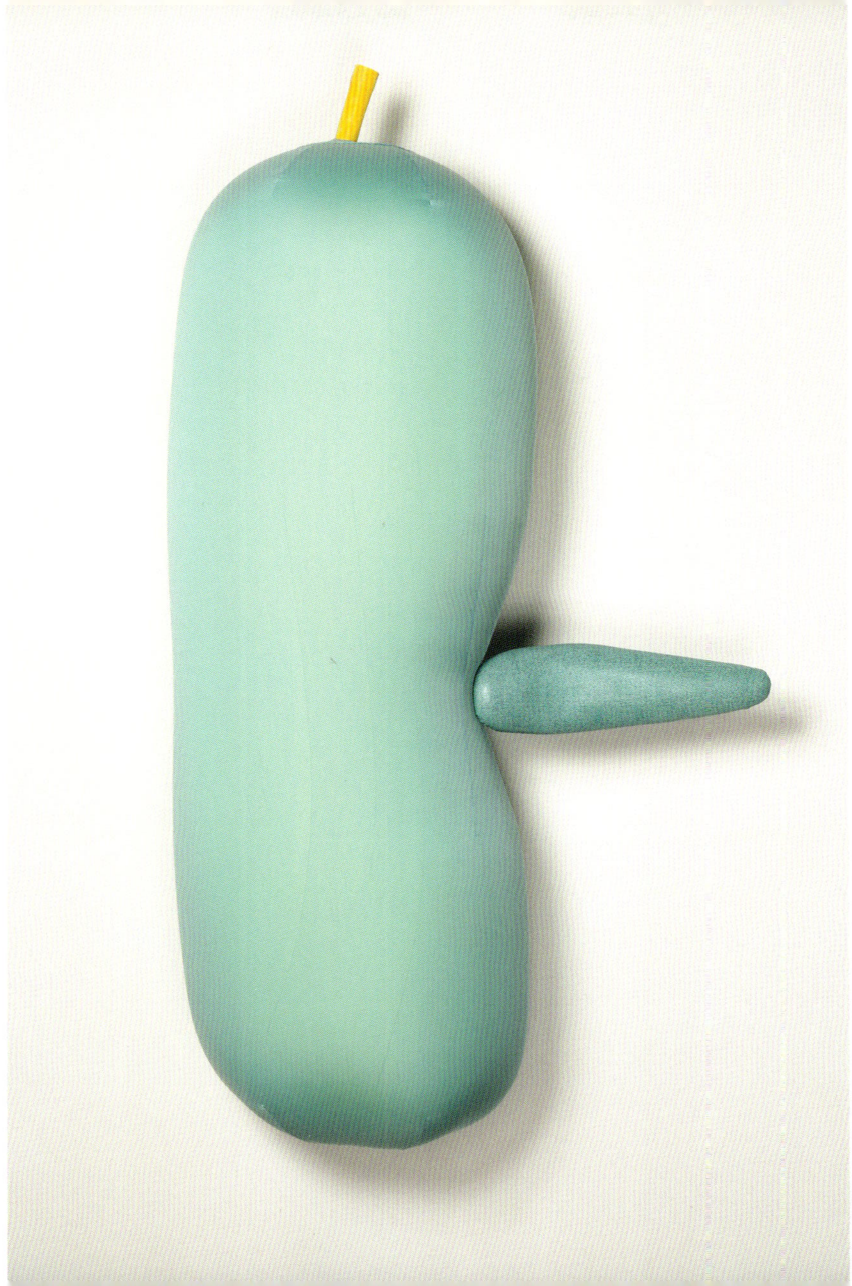

DUSTUP (2012), pp 29–33, 35, 41, 46–49, 57–59, 64–67

20′ x 20′ x 16′

vinyl-coated nylon, rope, leather, blowers, sandbags, sawdust;
installation size variable

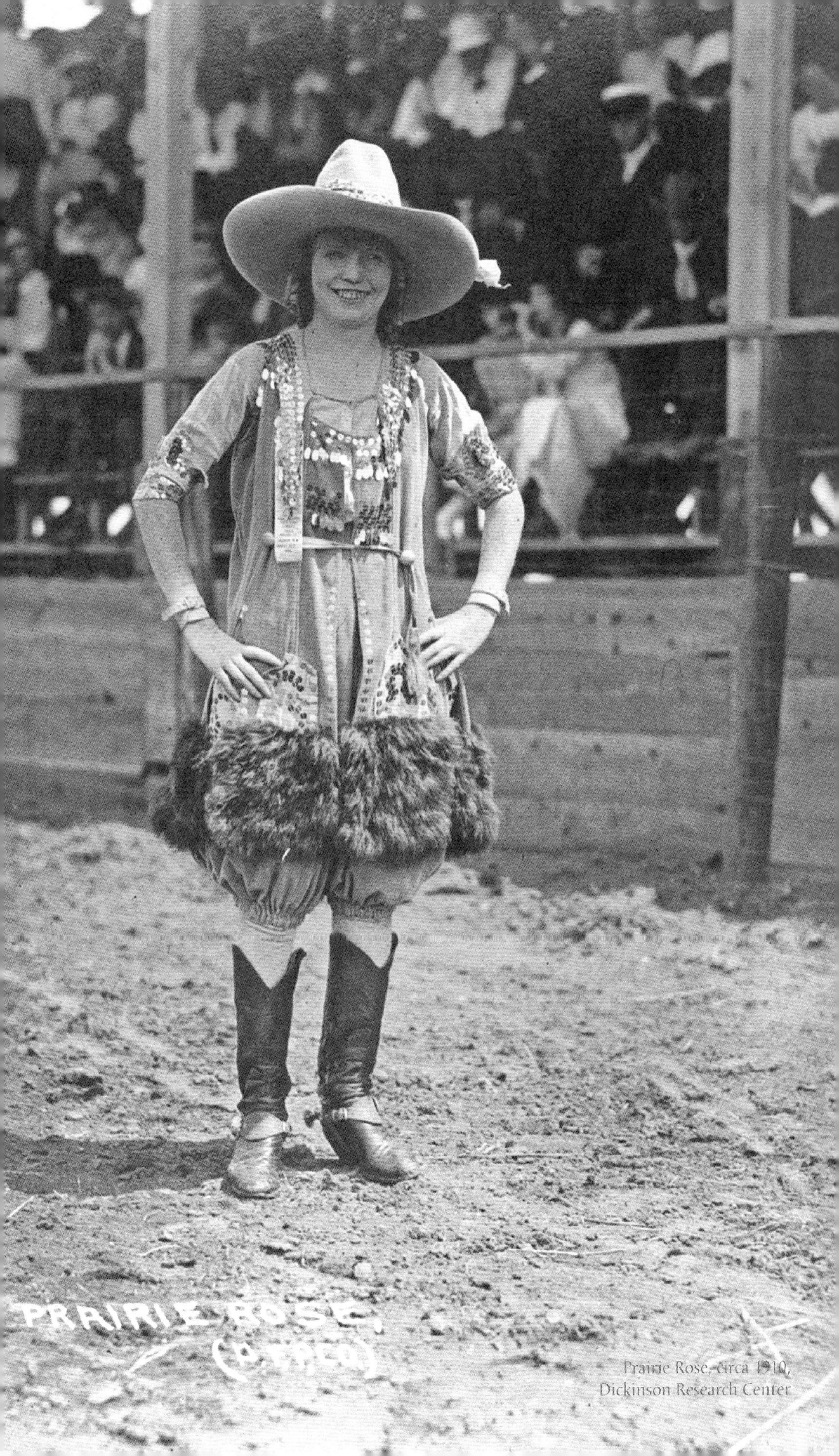

Prairie Rose, circa 1910,
Dickinson Research Center

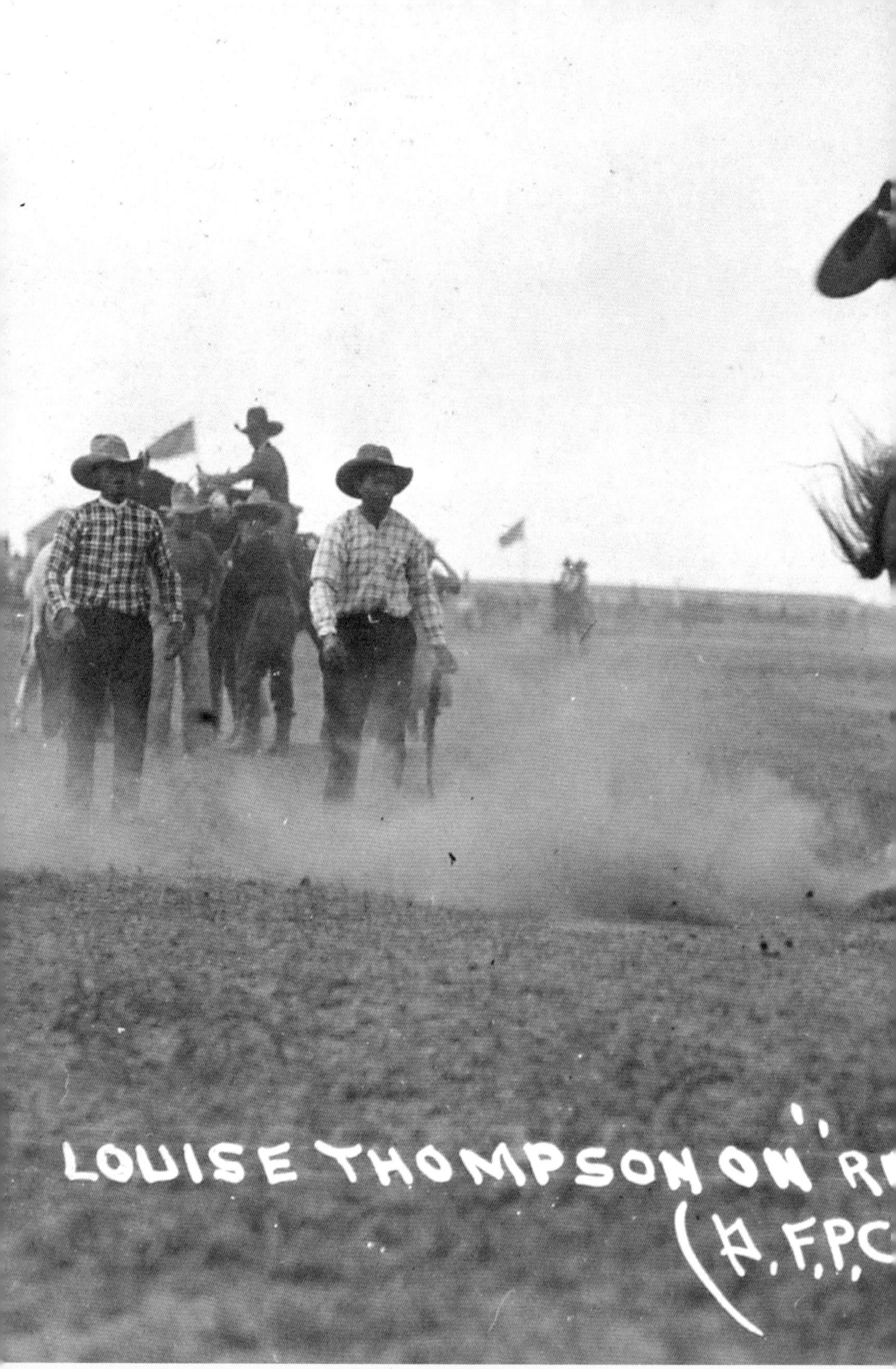

Louise Thompson, 1916, Autry National Center

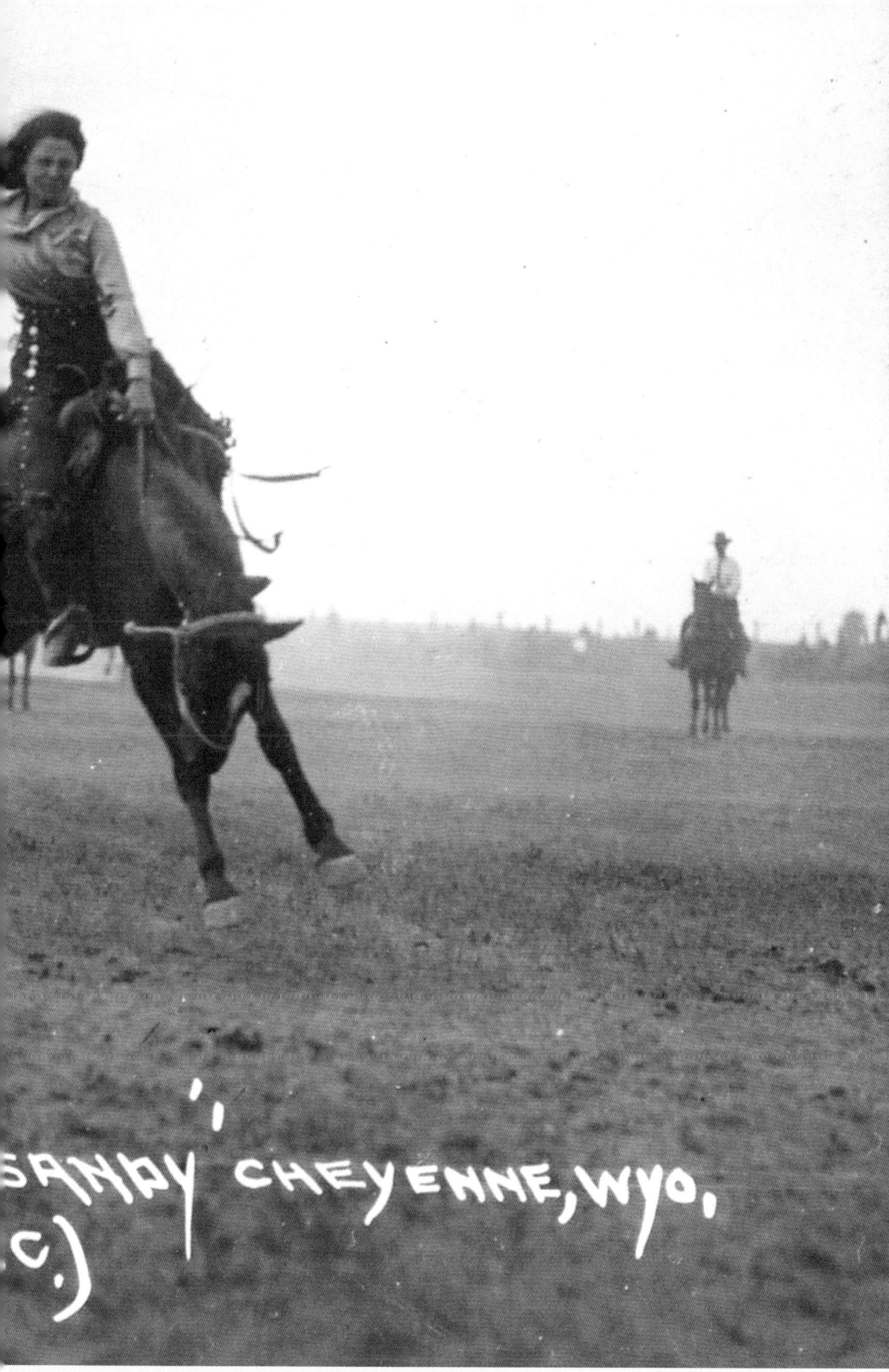
SANDY CHEYENNE, WYO.
C.)

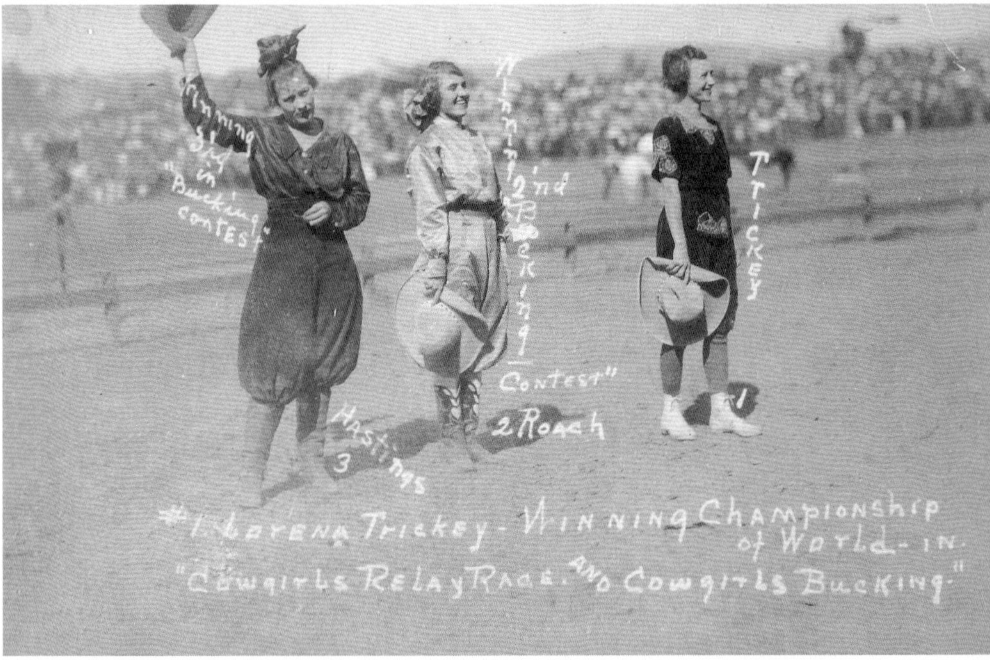

Lorena Trickey (right), winning world championship in cowgirls' relay race and cowgirls' bucking

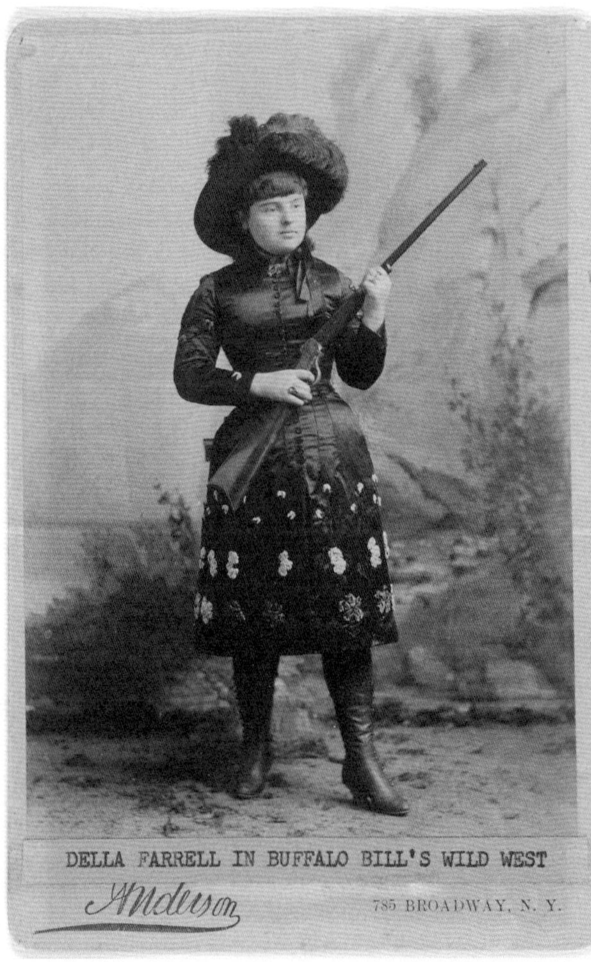

Della Farrell, Buffalo Bill's Wild West Show, Autry National Center

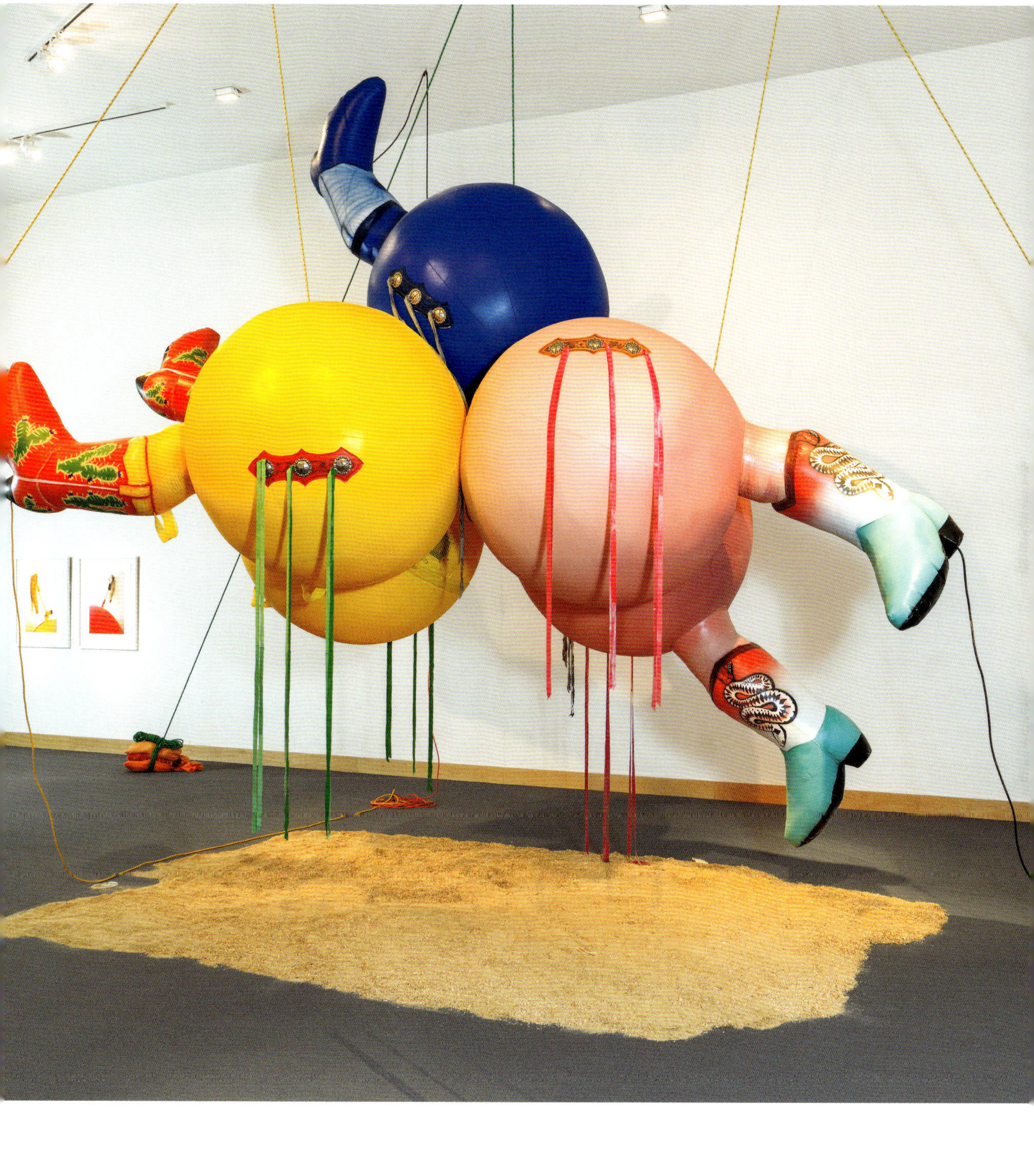

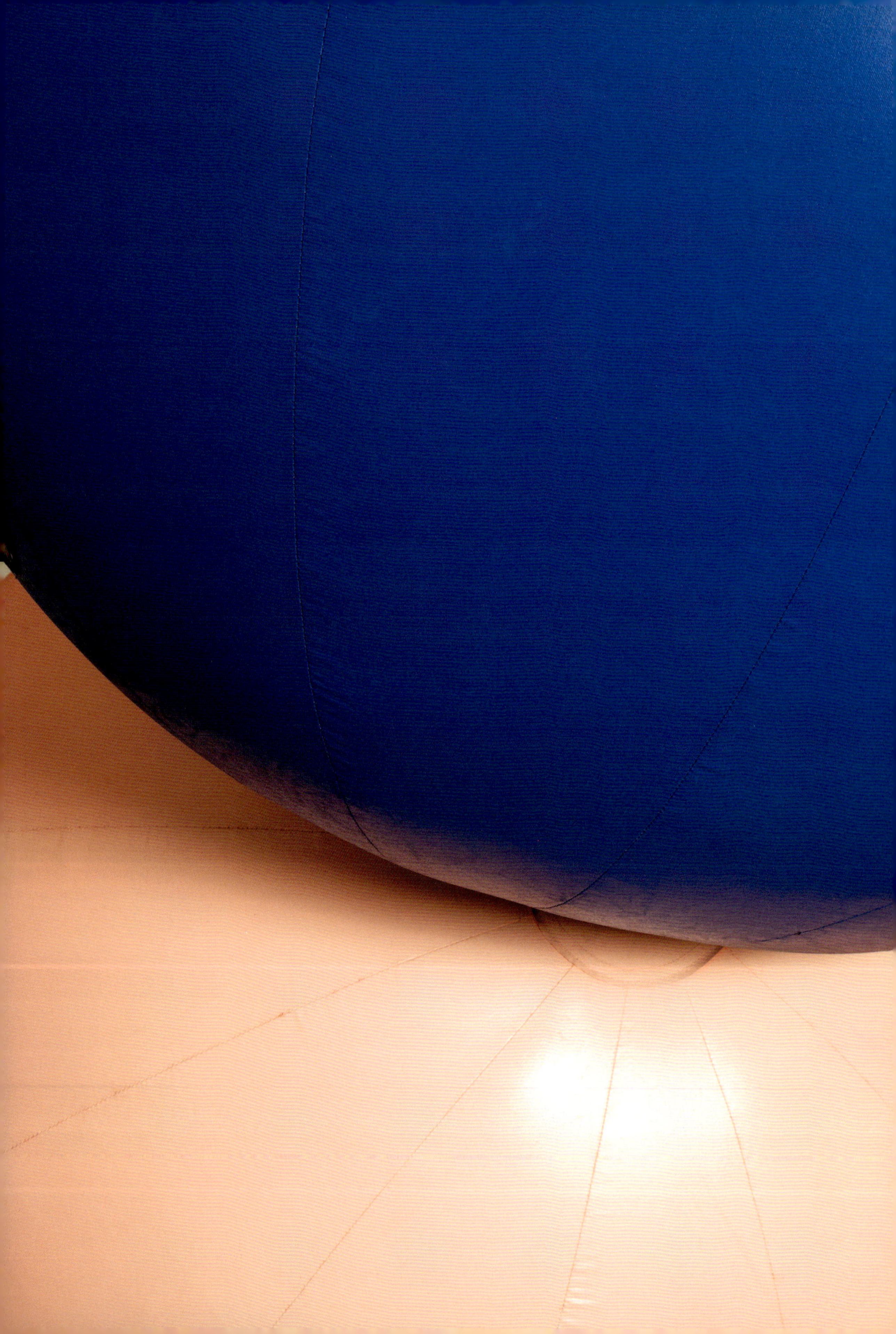

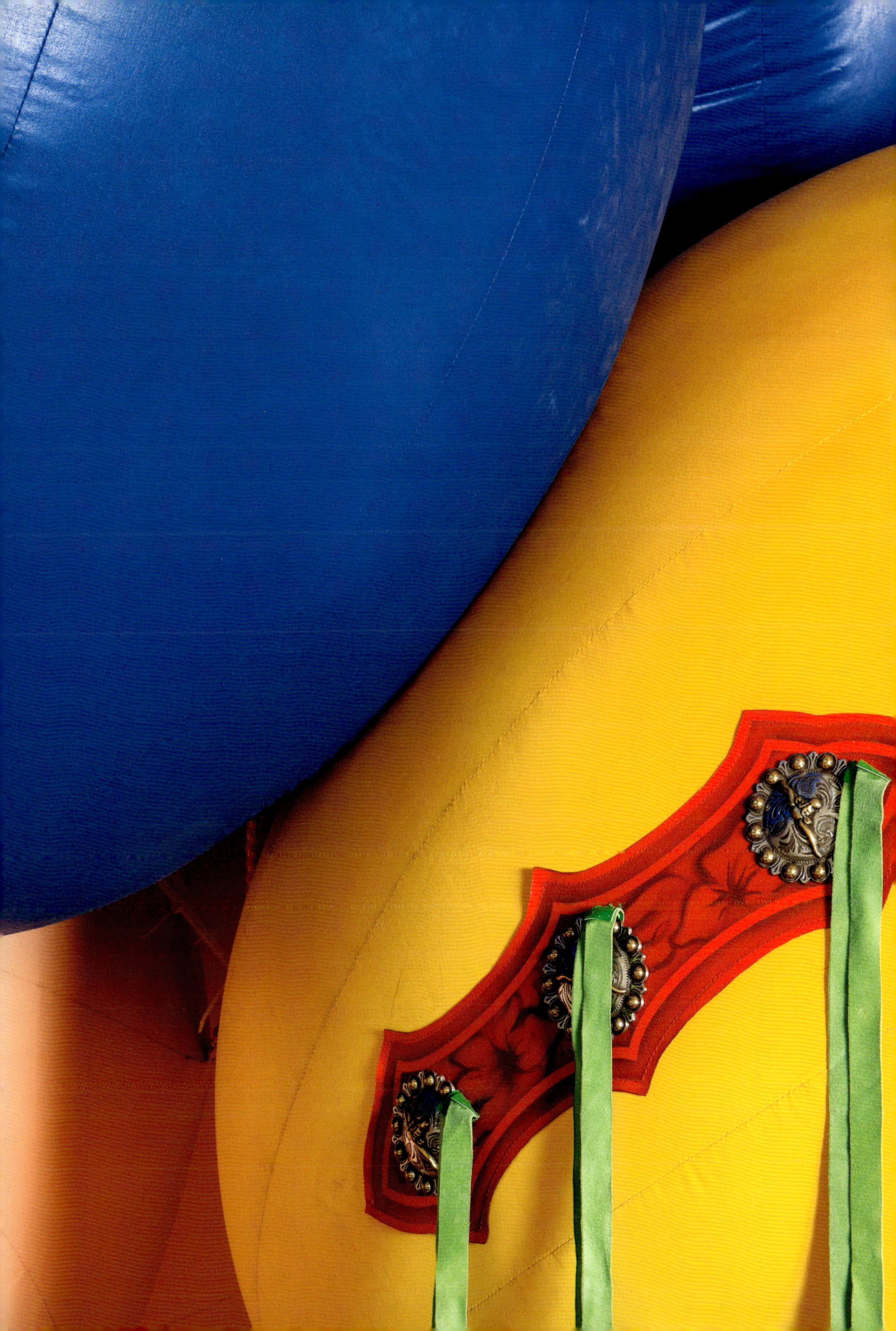

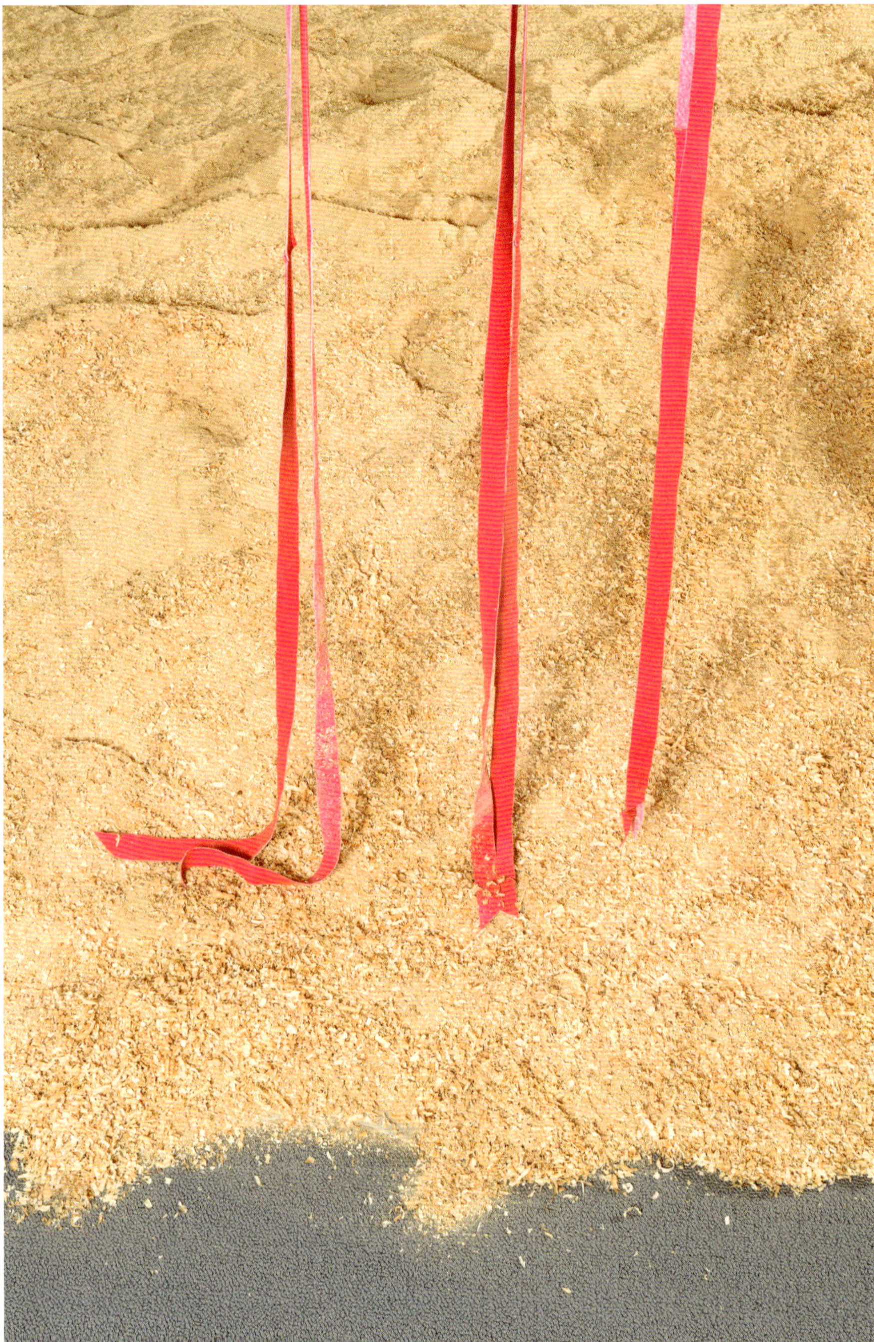

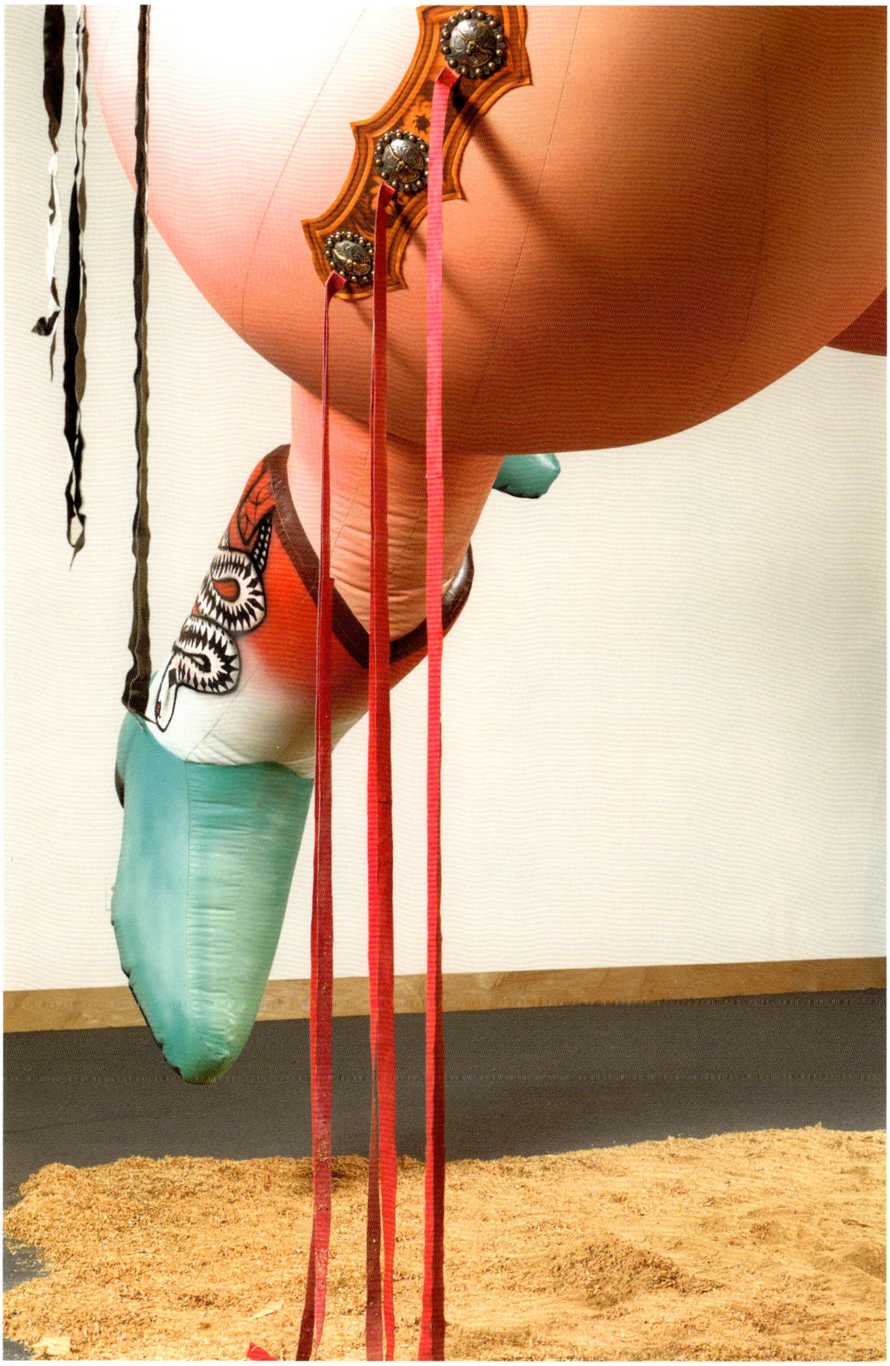

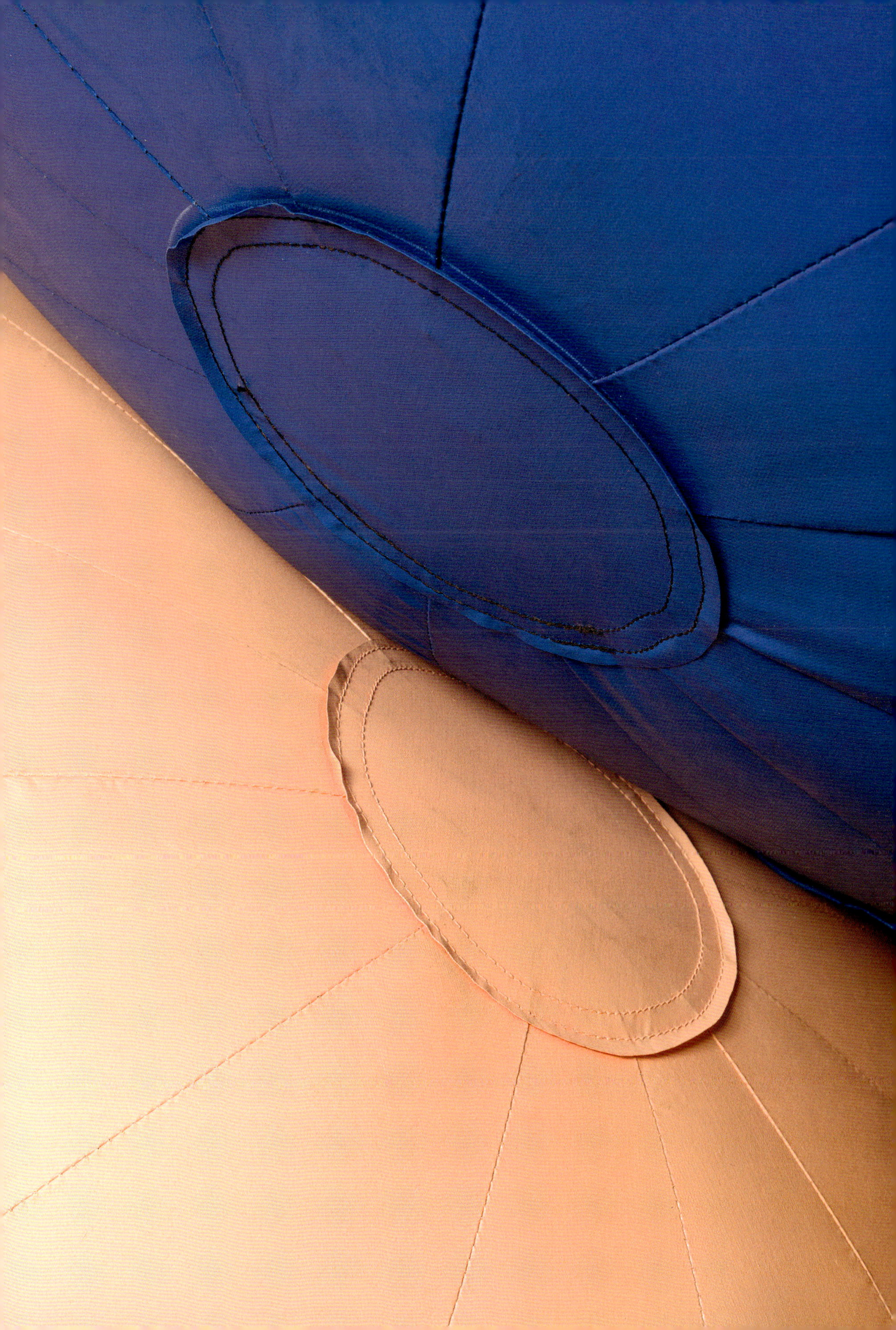

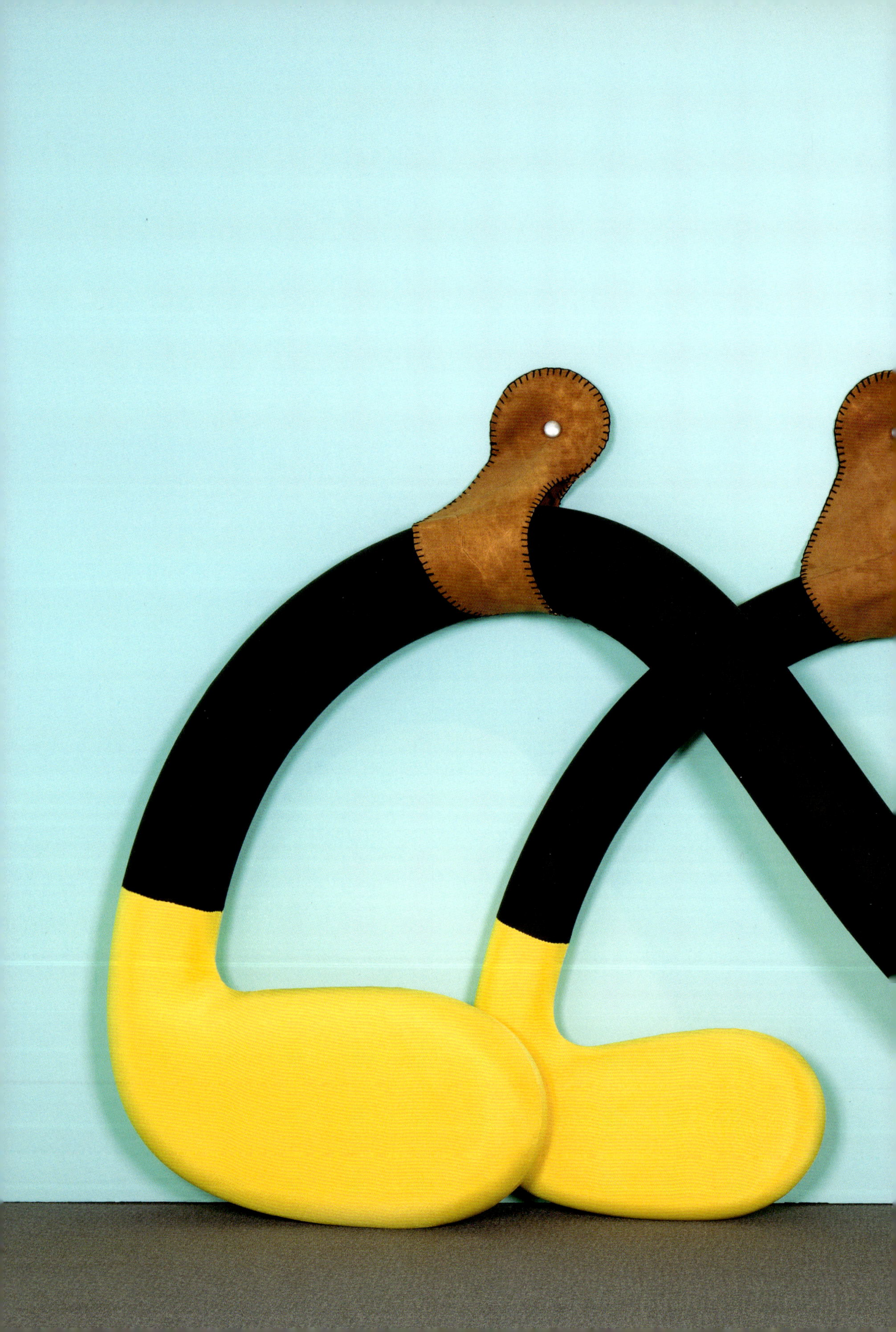

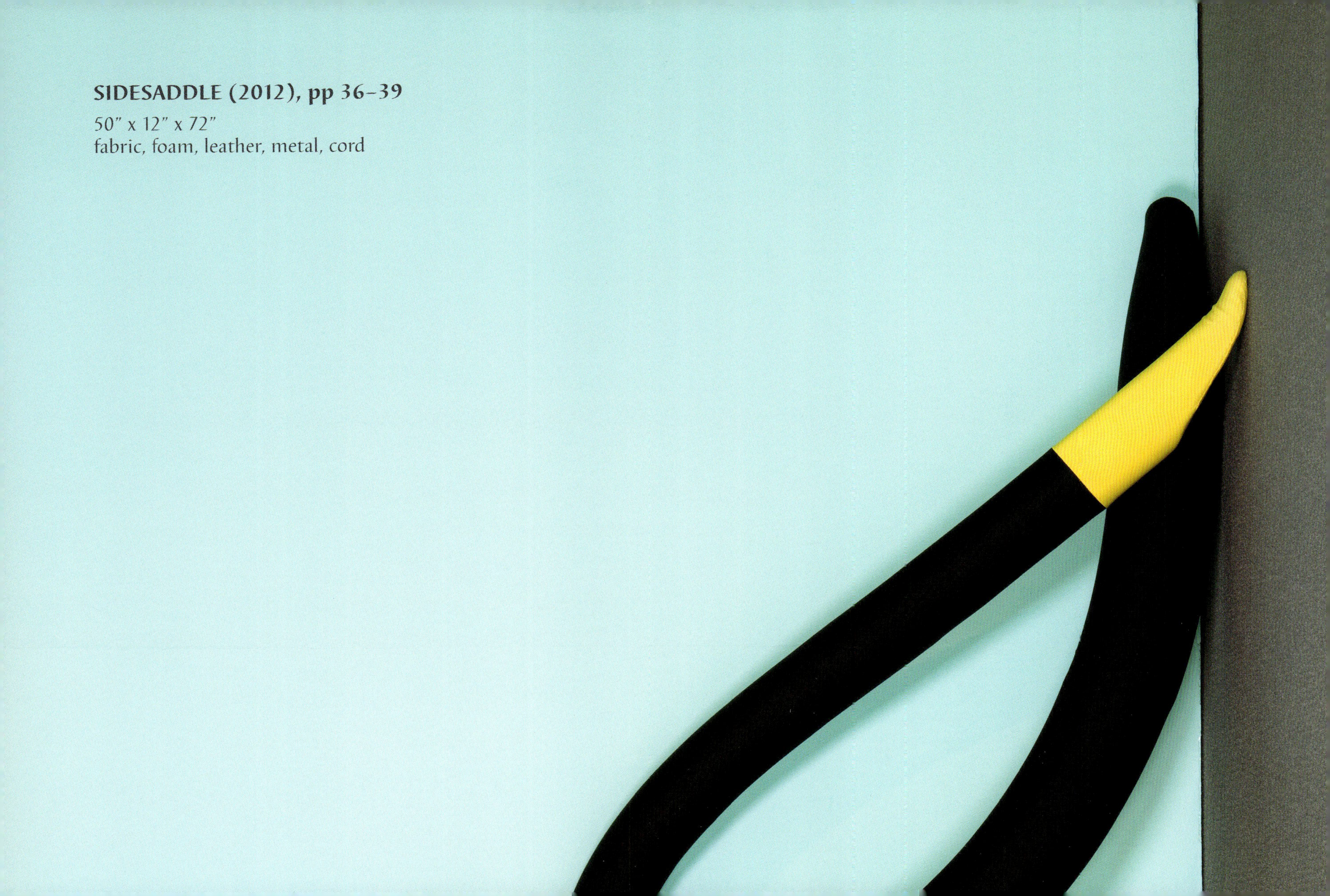

SIDESADDLE (2012), pp 36–39
50" x 12" x 72"
fabric, foam, leather, metal, cord

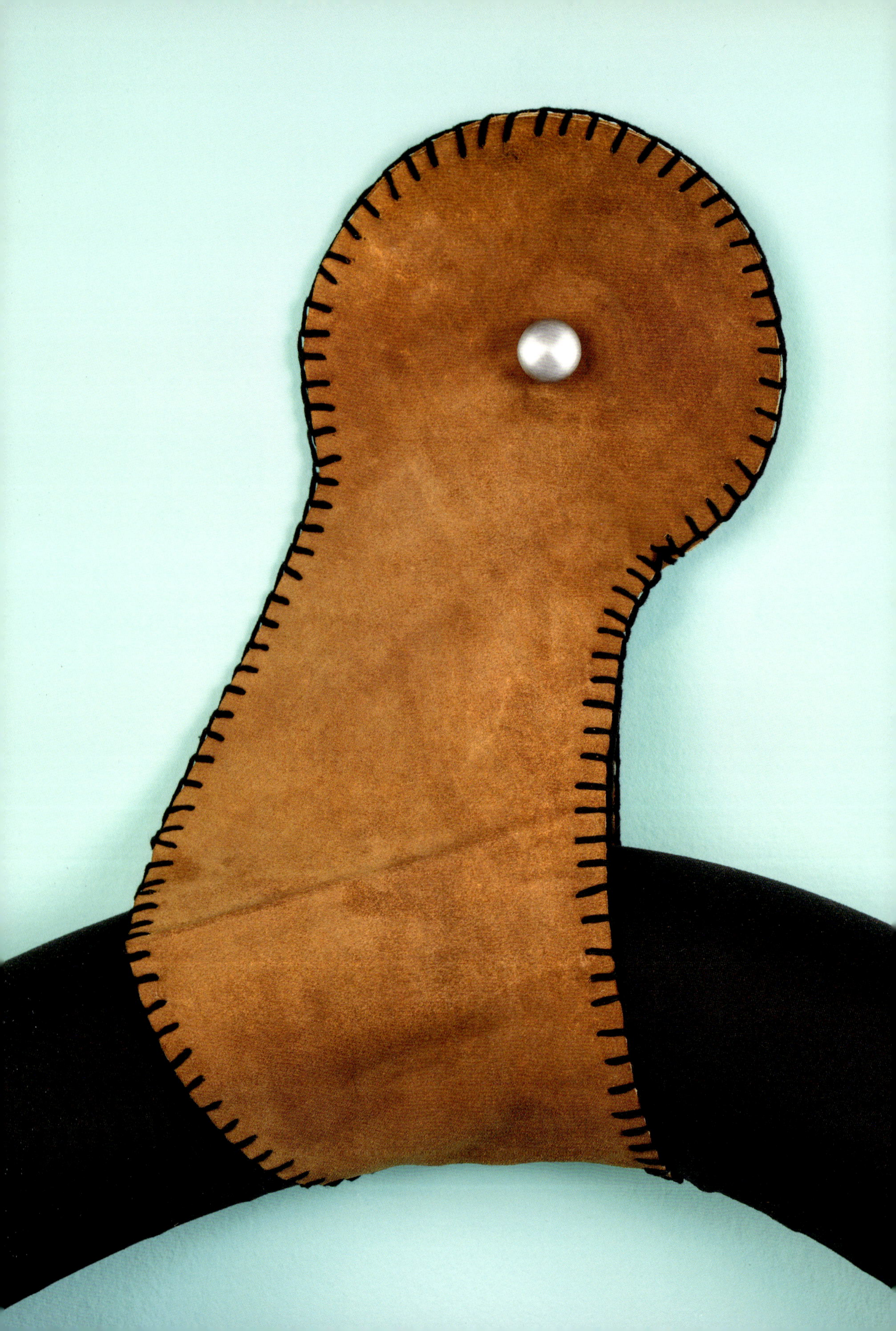

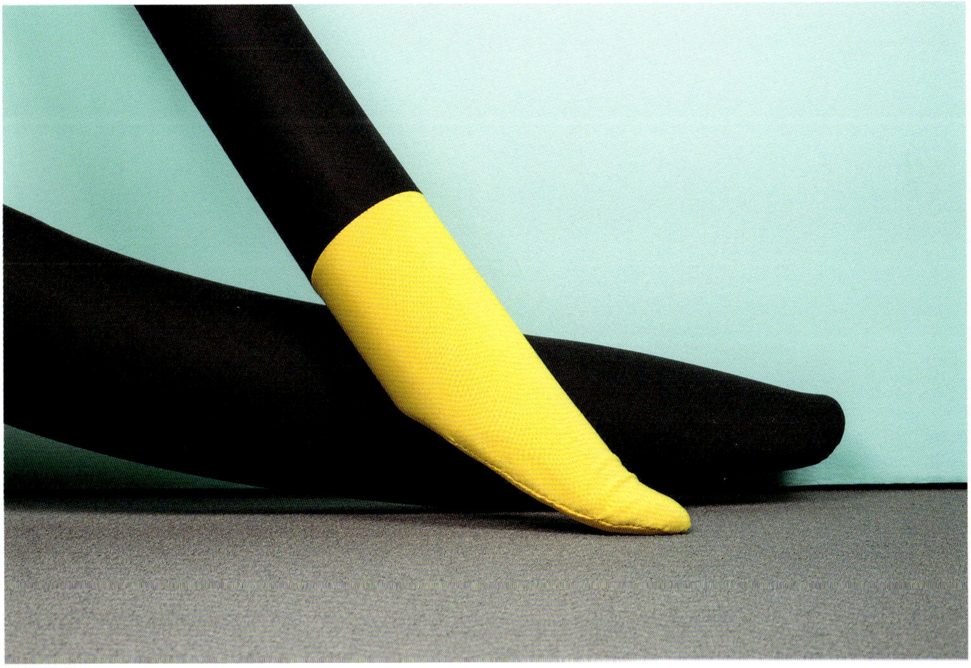

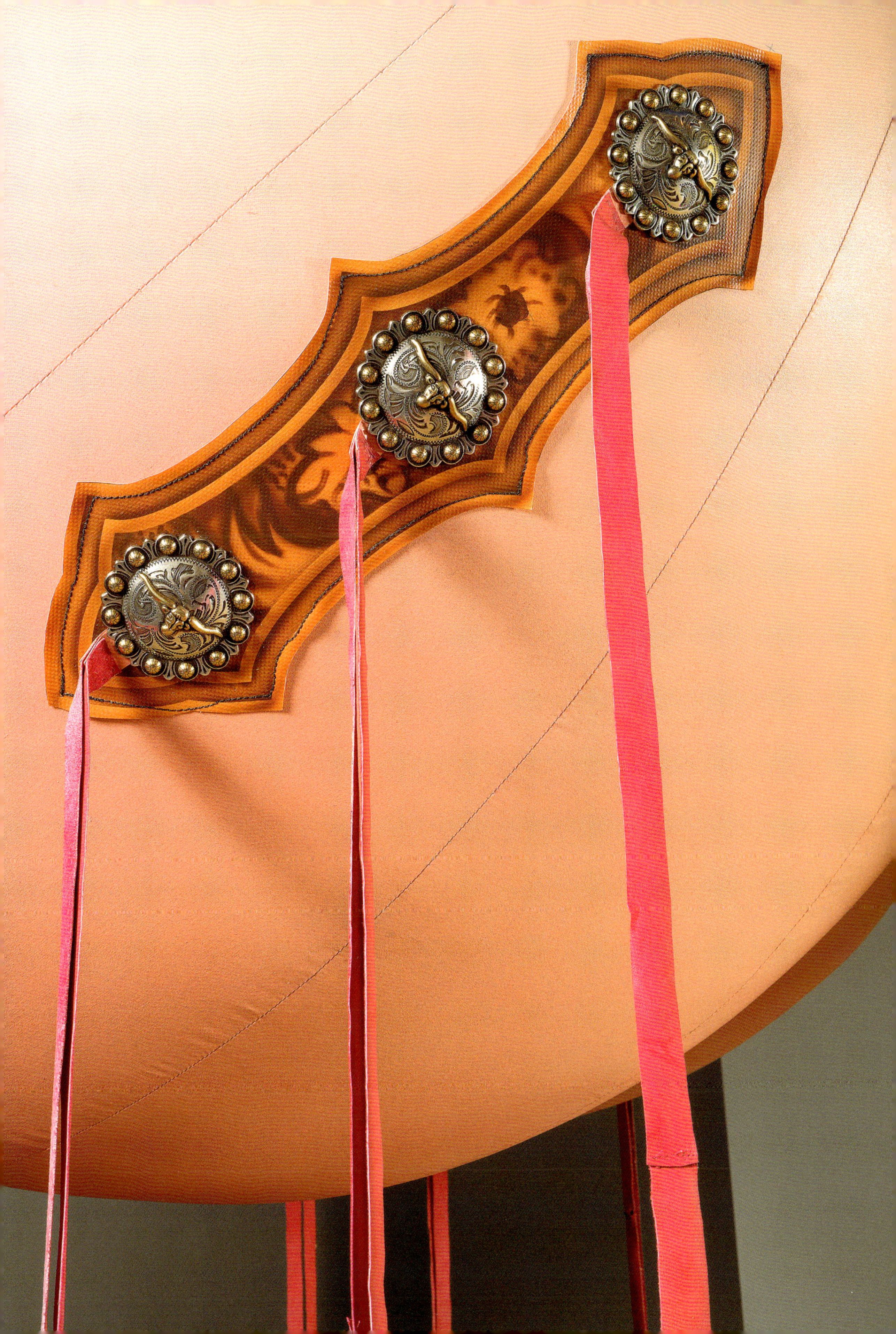

STRAPPED-ON (2007), pp 43–45

52″ x 26″ x 60″
latex, fabric, wood, rope

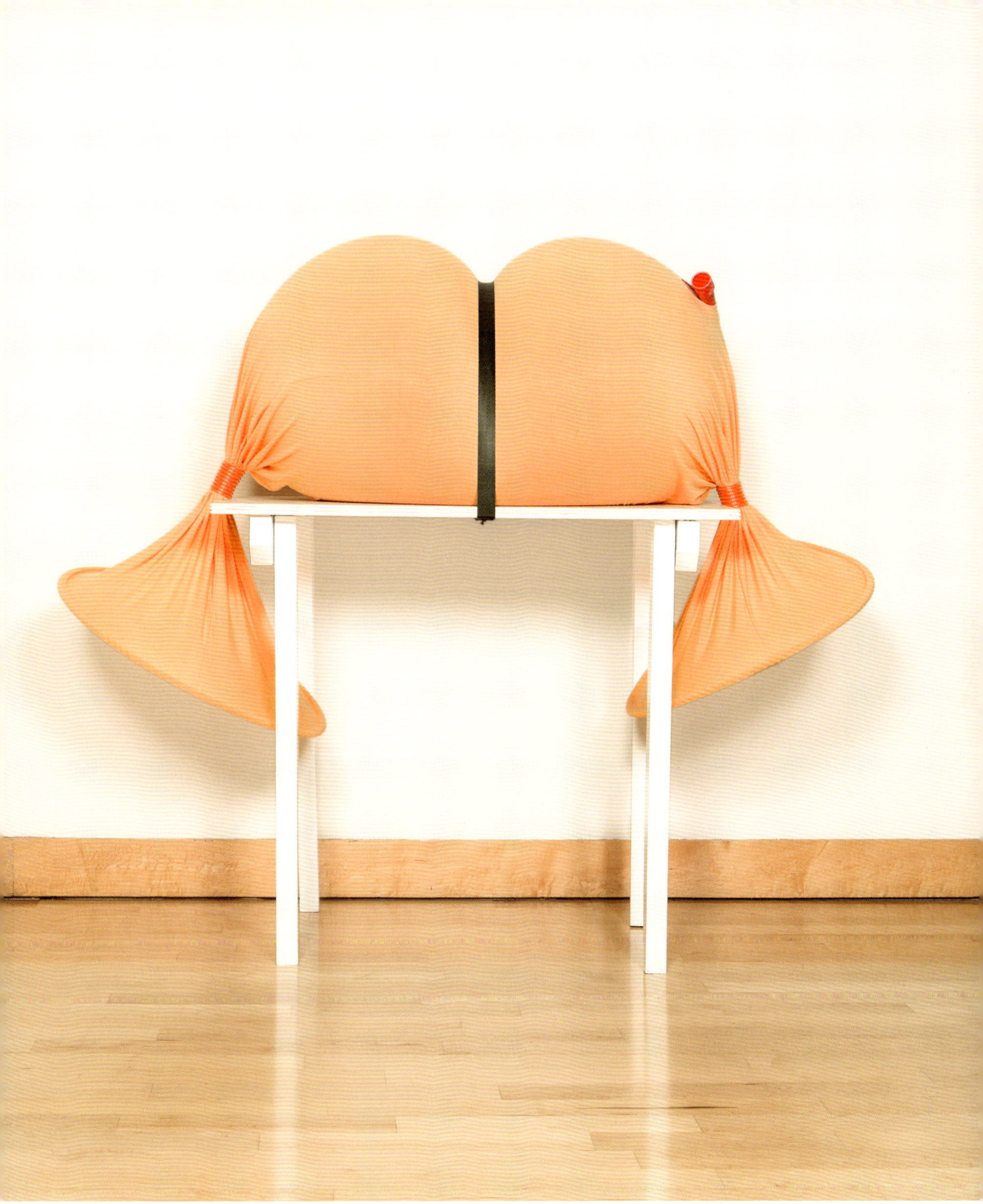

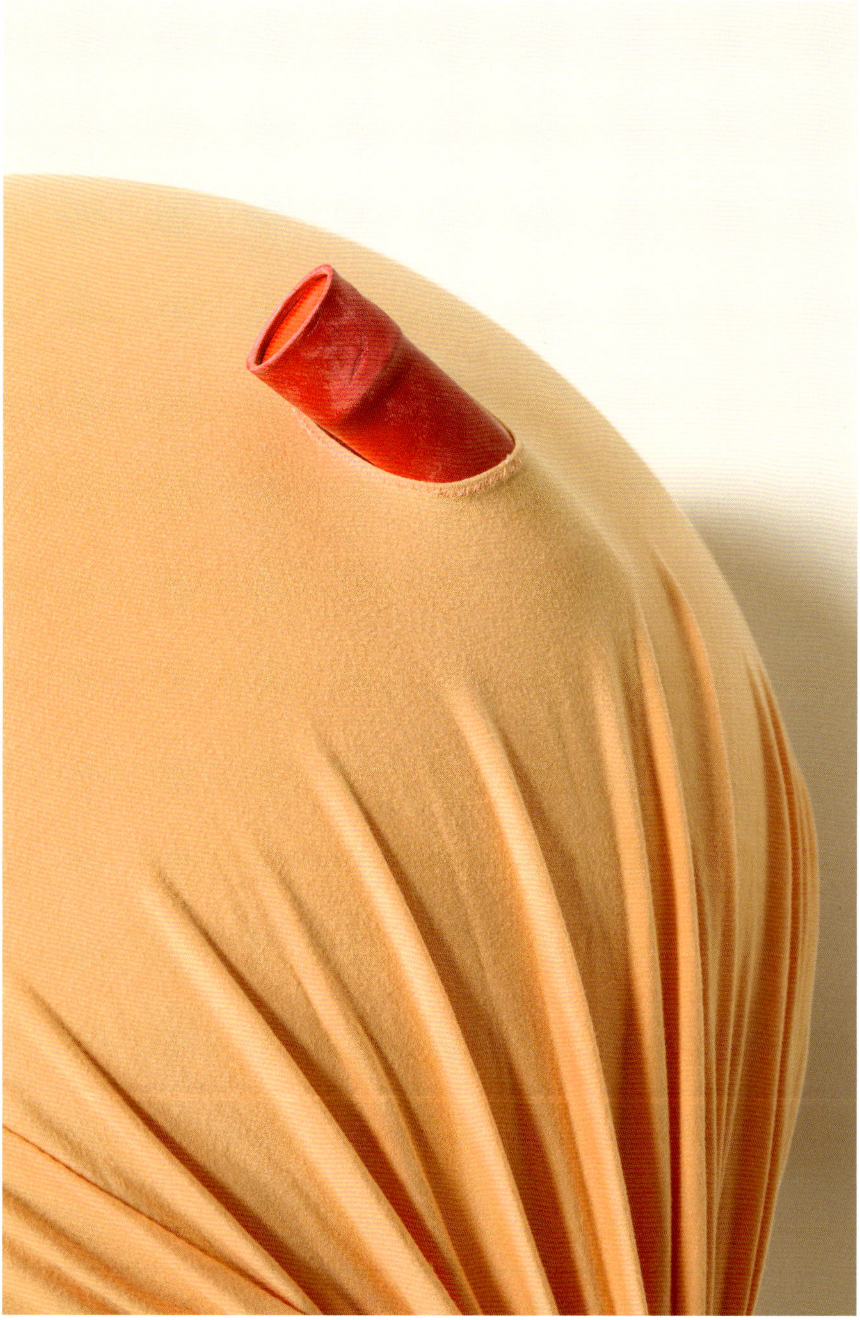

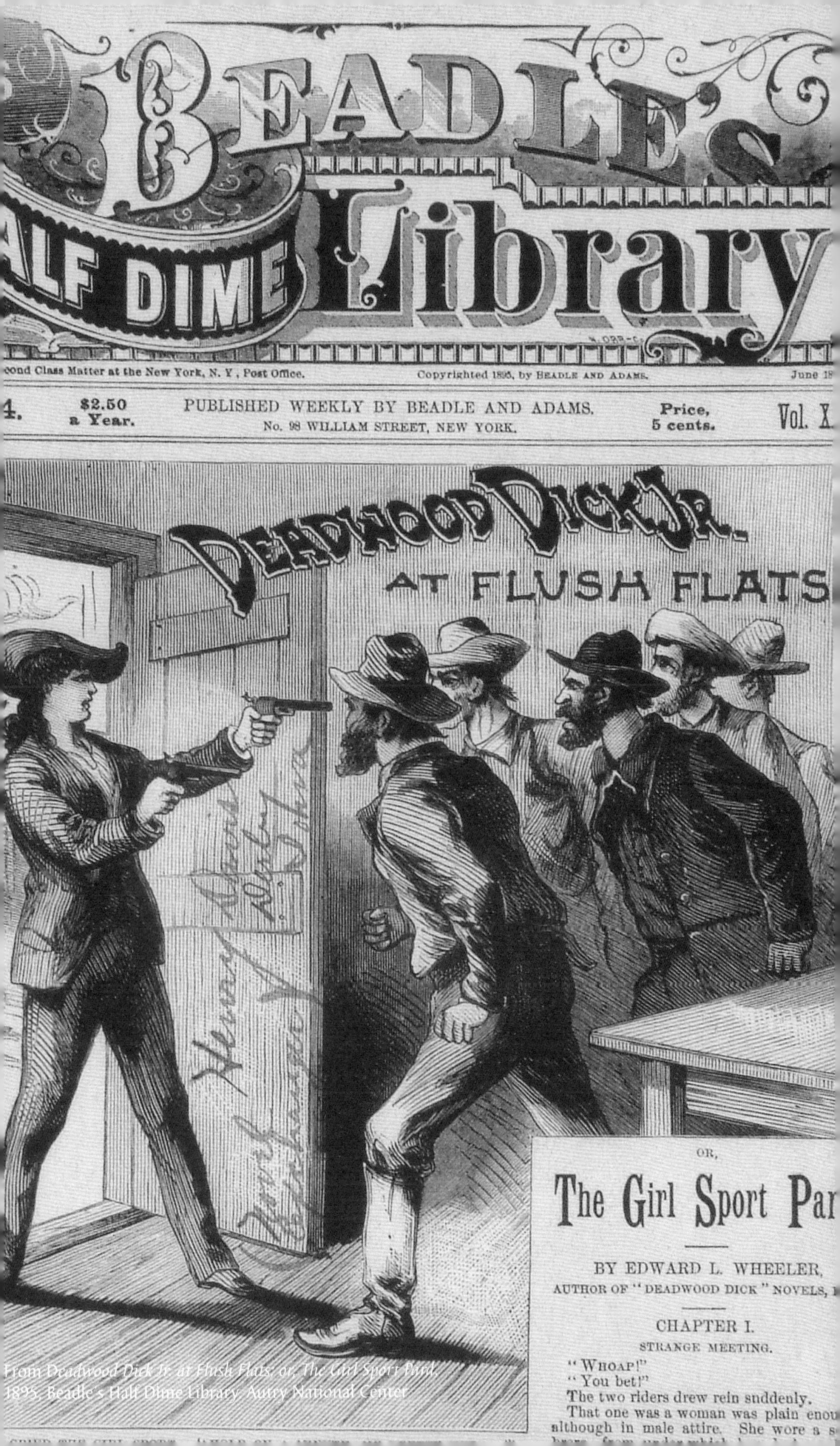

BEADLE'S HALF DIME Library

ond Class Matter at the New York, N. Y., Post Office. Copyrighted 1895, by BEADLE AND ADAMS. June 18

4. $2.50 a Year. PUBLISHED WEEKLY BY BEADLE AND ADAMS. No. 98 WILLIAM STREET, NEW YORK. Price, 5 cents. Vol. X

DEADWOOD DICK JR.

AT FLUSH FLATS

OR,

The Girl Sport Par

BY EDWARD L. WHEELER,

AUTHOR OF "DEADWOOD DICK" NOVELS, E

CHAPTER I.

STRANGE MEETING.

"WHOAP!"

"You bet!"

The two riders drew rein suddenly.

That one was a woman was plain enou although in male attire. She wore a s

From *Deadwood Dick Jr. at Flush Flats; or, The Girl Sport Pard.* 1895, Beadle's Half Dime Library. Autry National Center

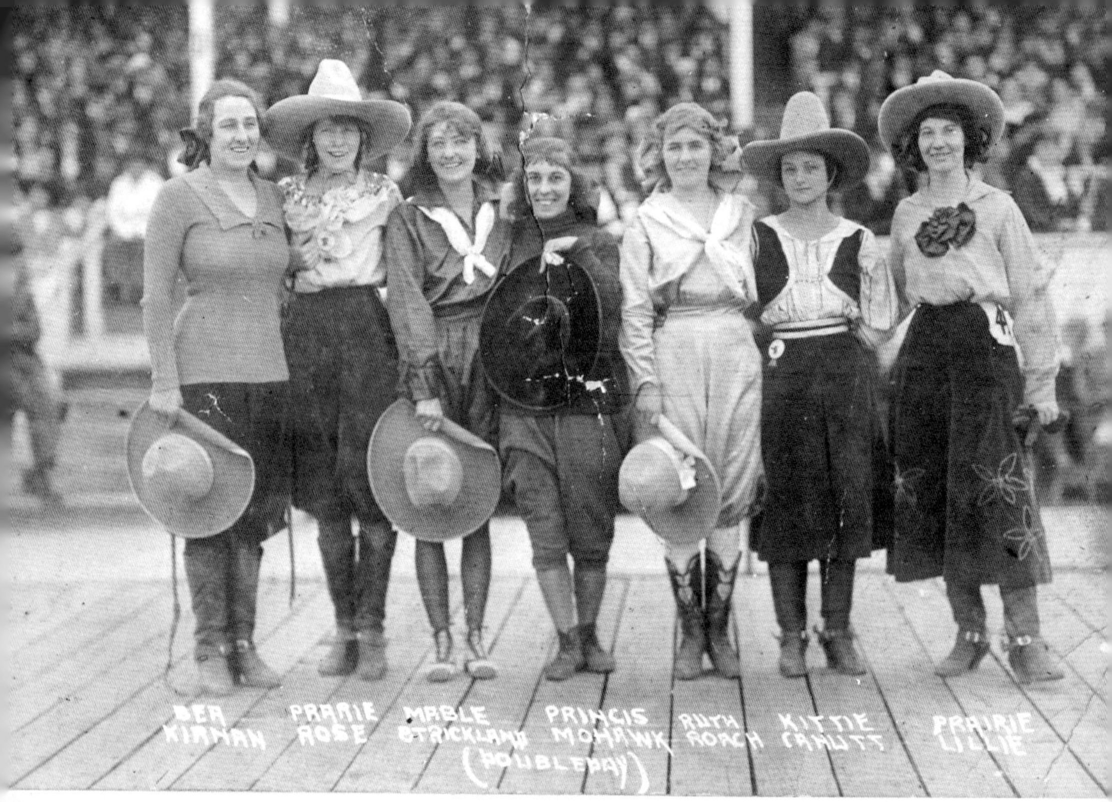

Left to right: Bea Kirnan, Prairie Rose, Mabel Strickland, Princess Mohawk, Ruth Roach, Kittie Canutt, and Prairie Lillie; Doubleday, 1920, Autry National Center

Left to right: Fox Hastings, Ruth Roach, Bea Kirnan, Florence Randolph, Rose Smith, and Mabel Strickland; Doubleday, 1930, Dickinson Research Center

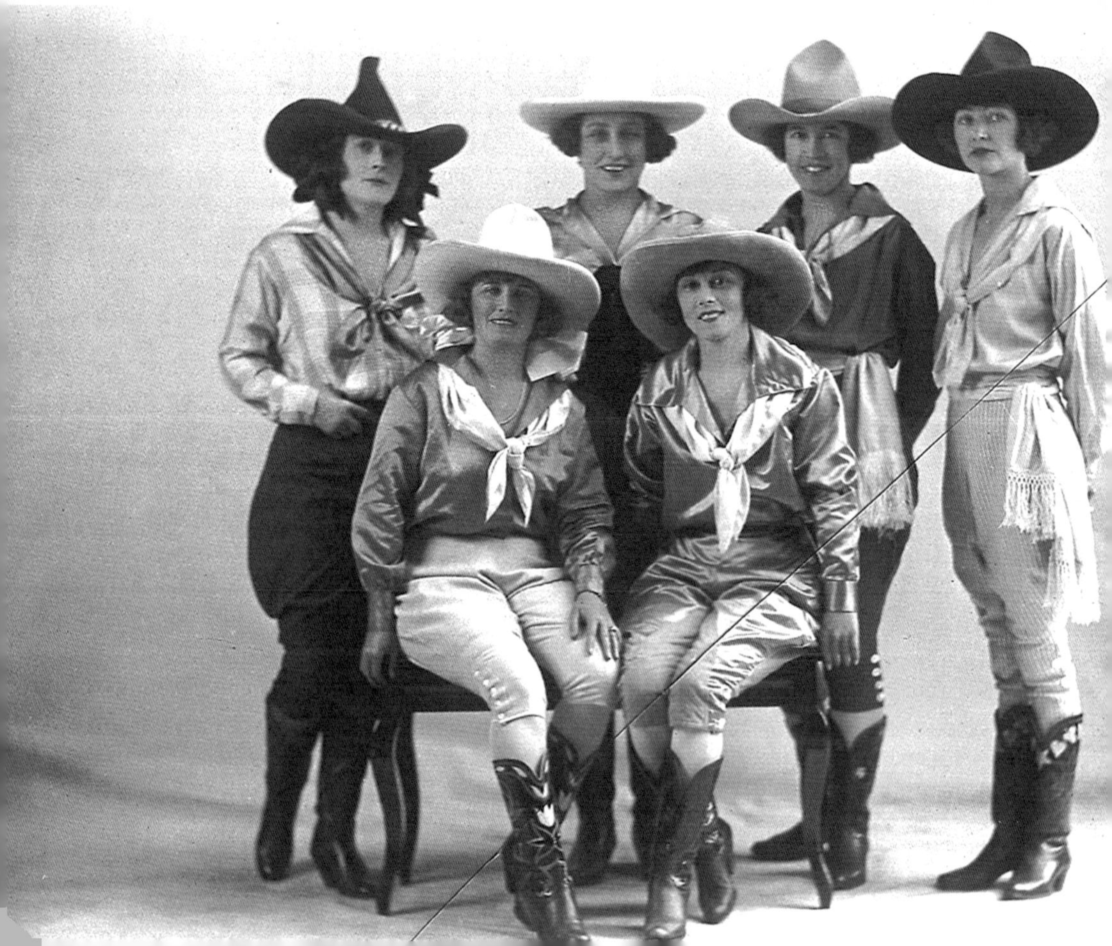

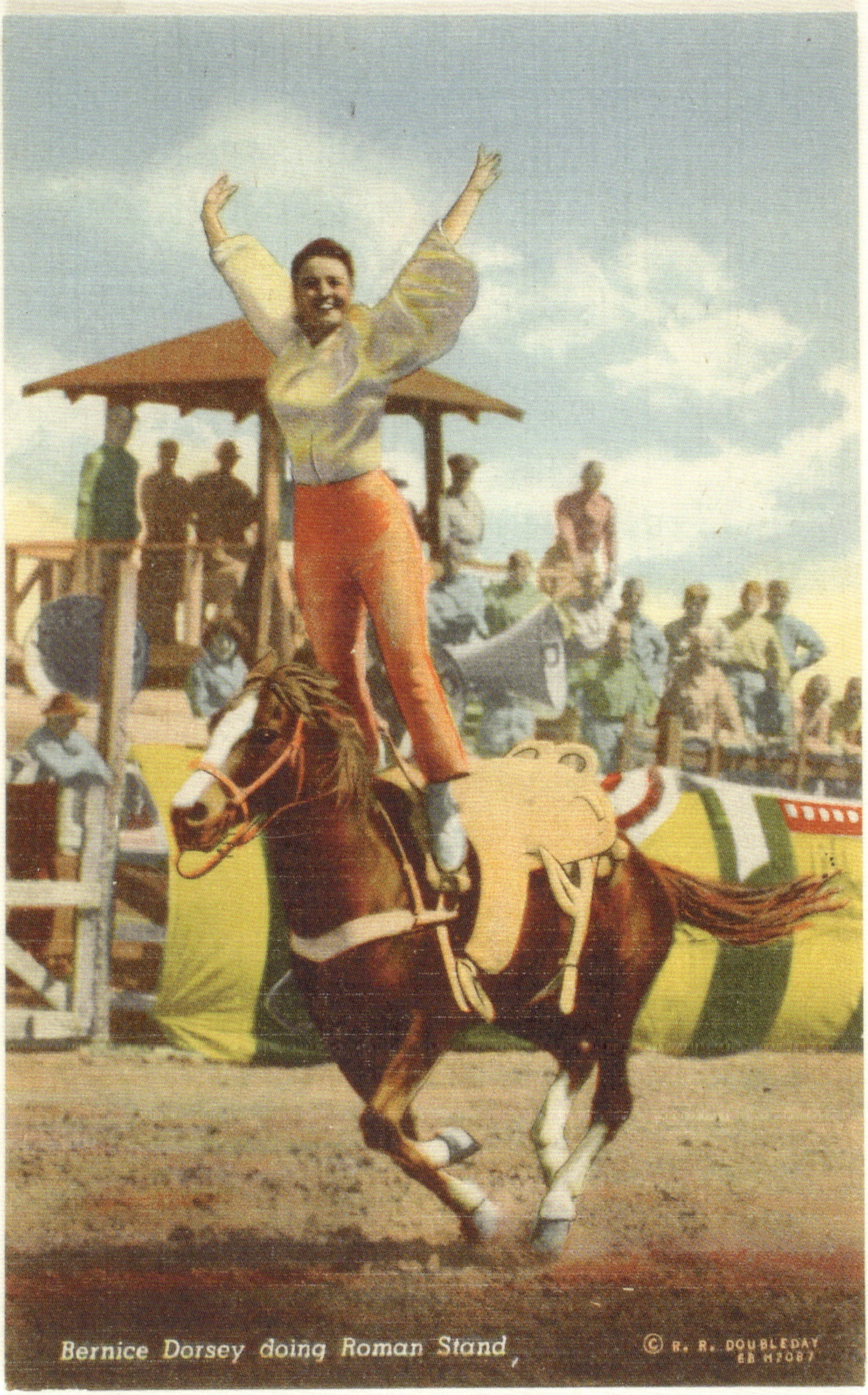

Bernice Dorsey doing Roman stand, Doubleday, 1948, Autry National Center

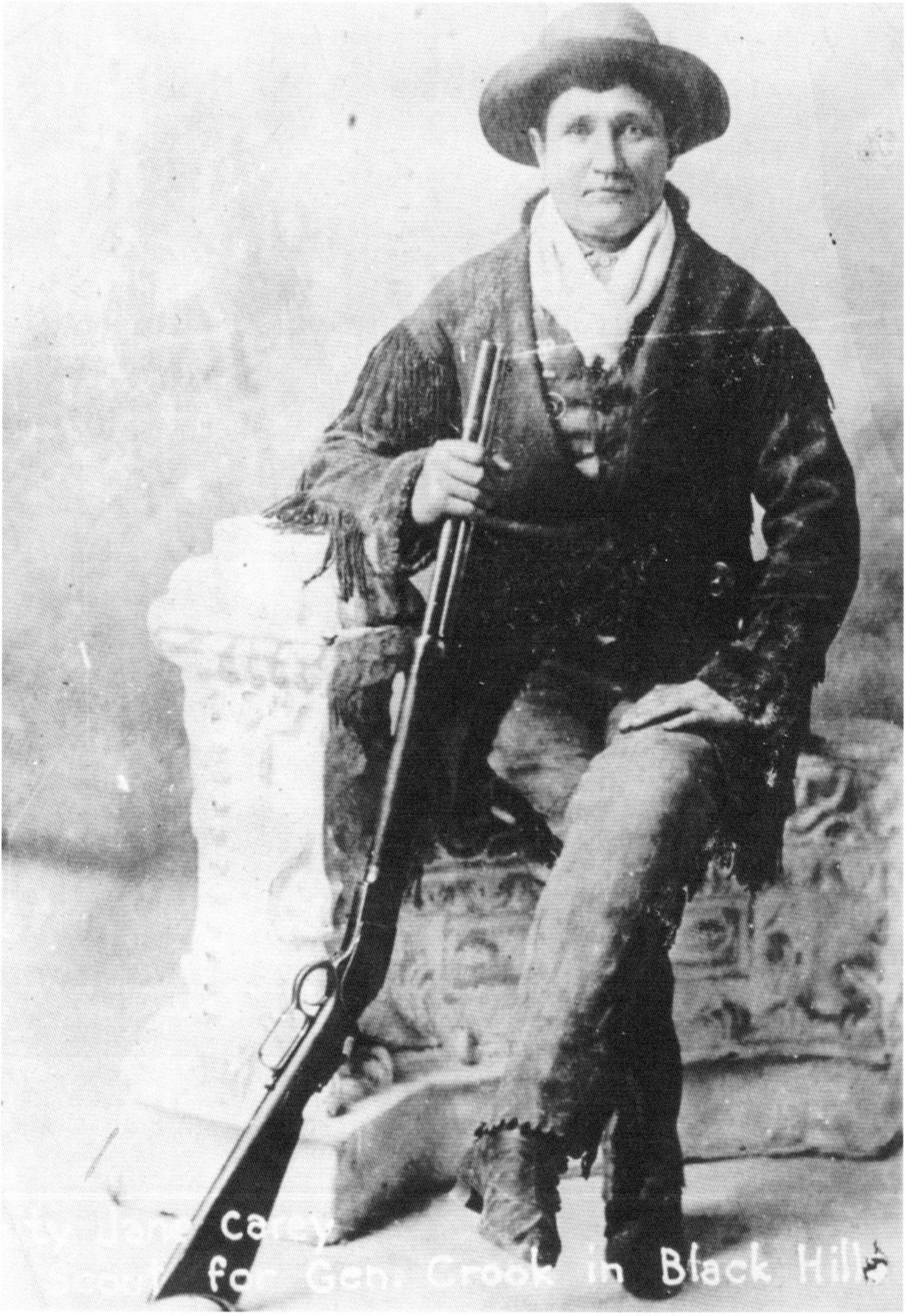

Calamity Jane Carey, as scout for Gen. Crook, 1880–1900, Autry National Center

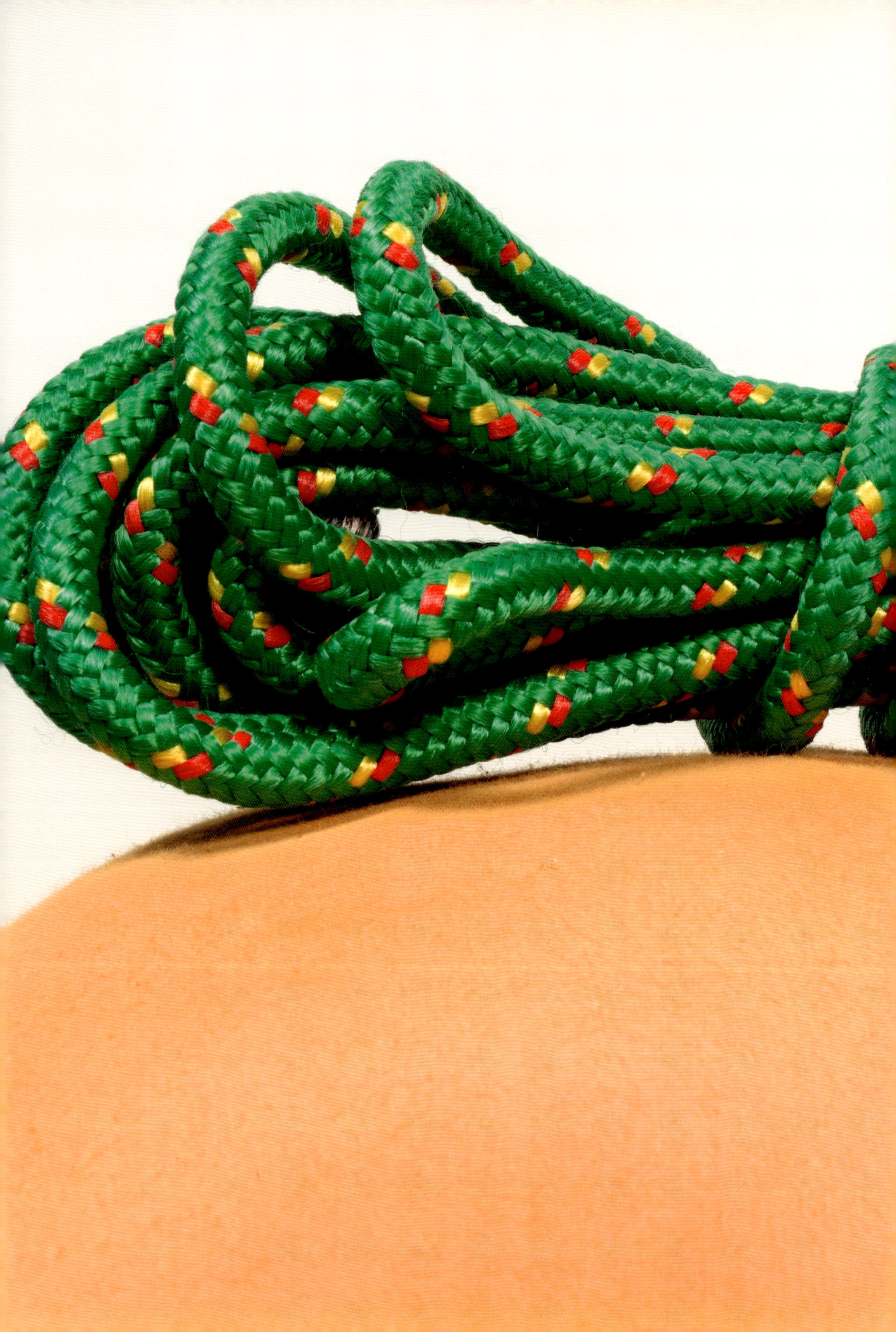

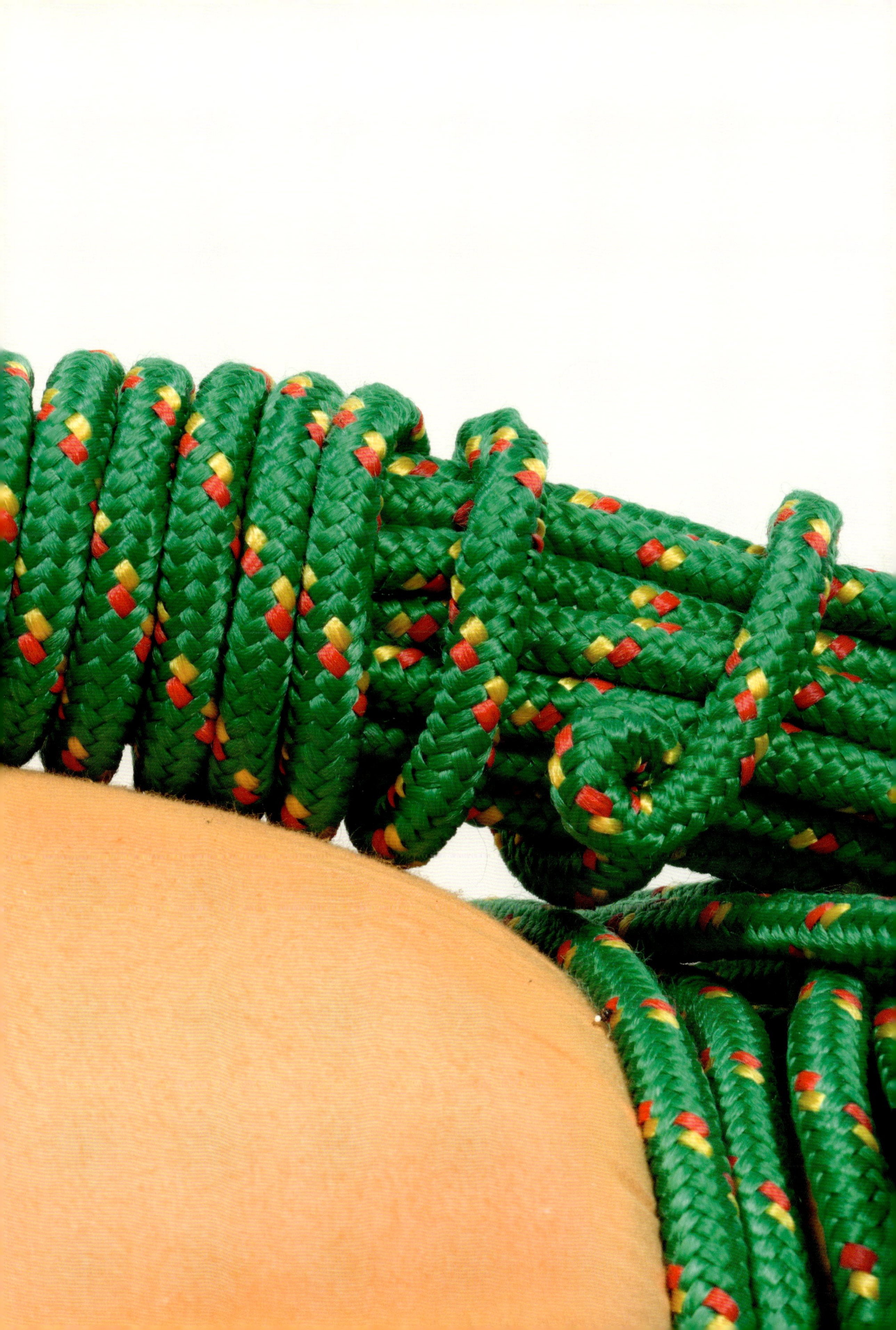

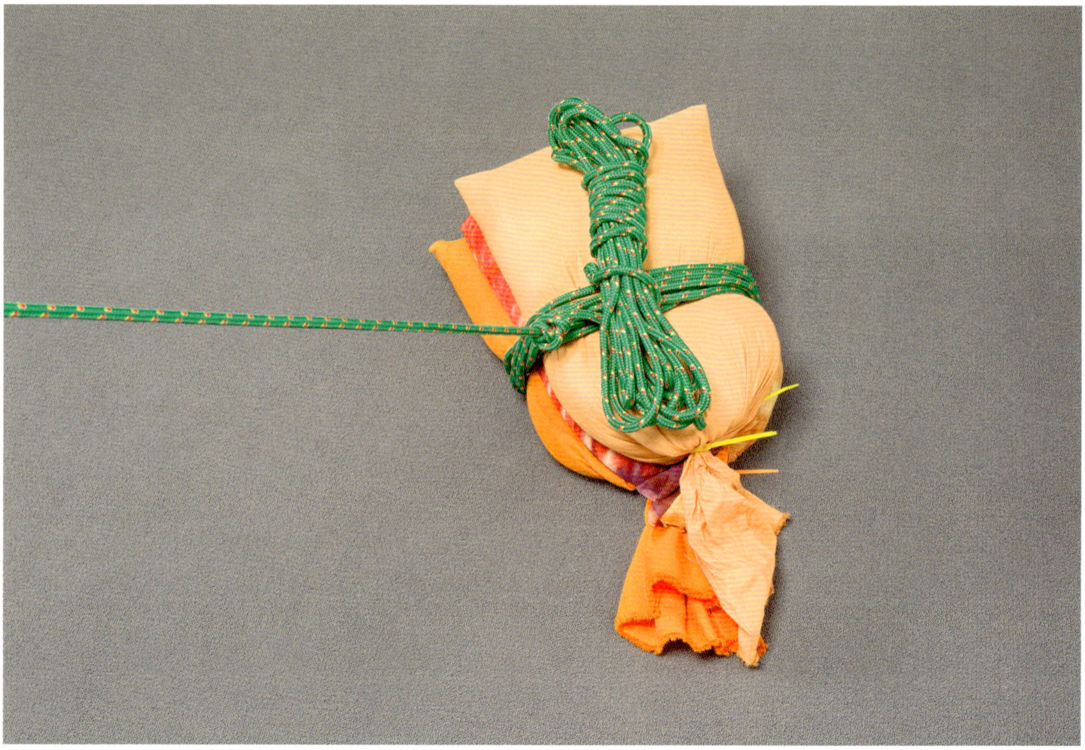

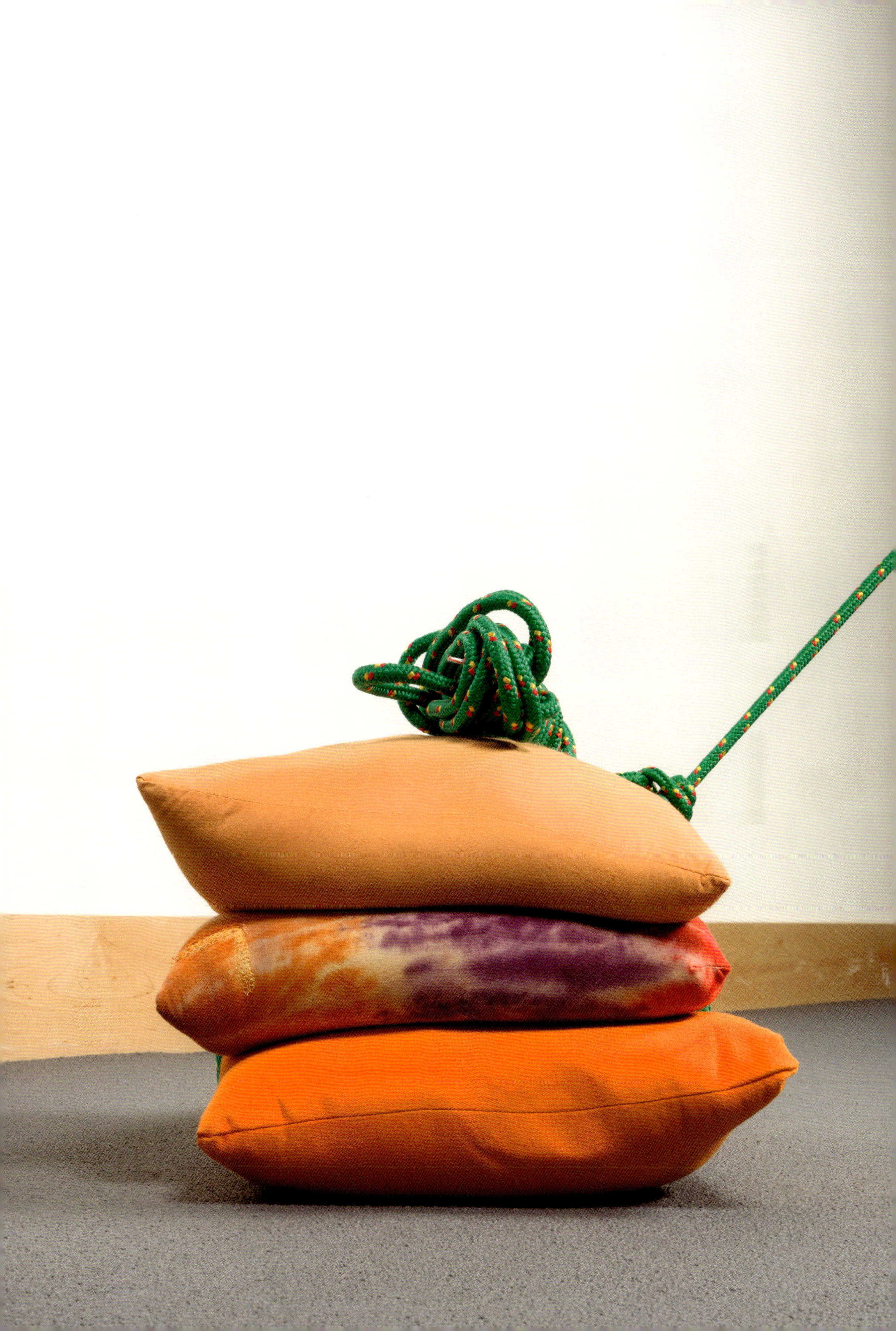

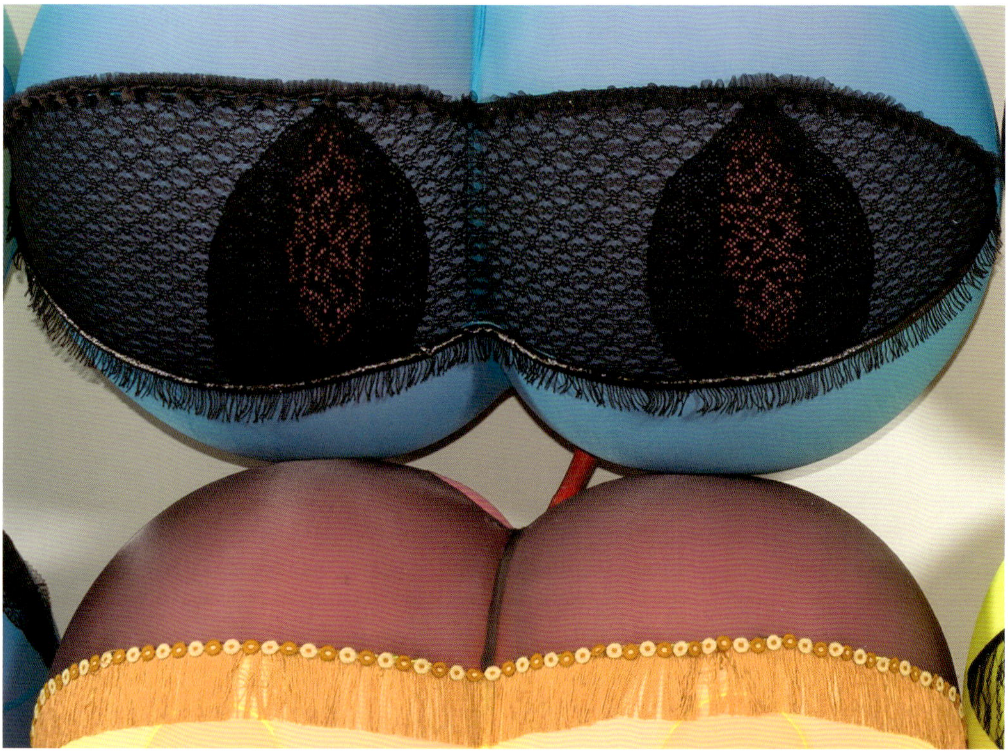

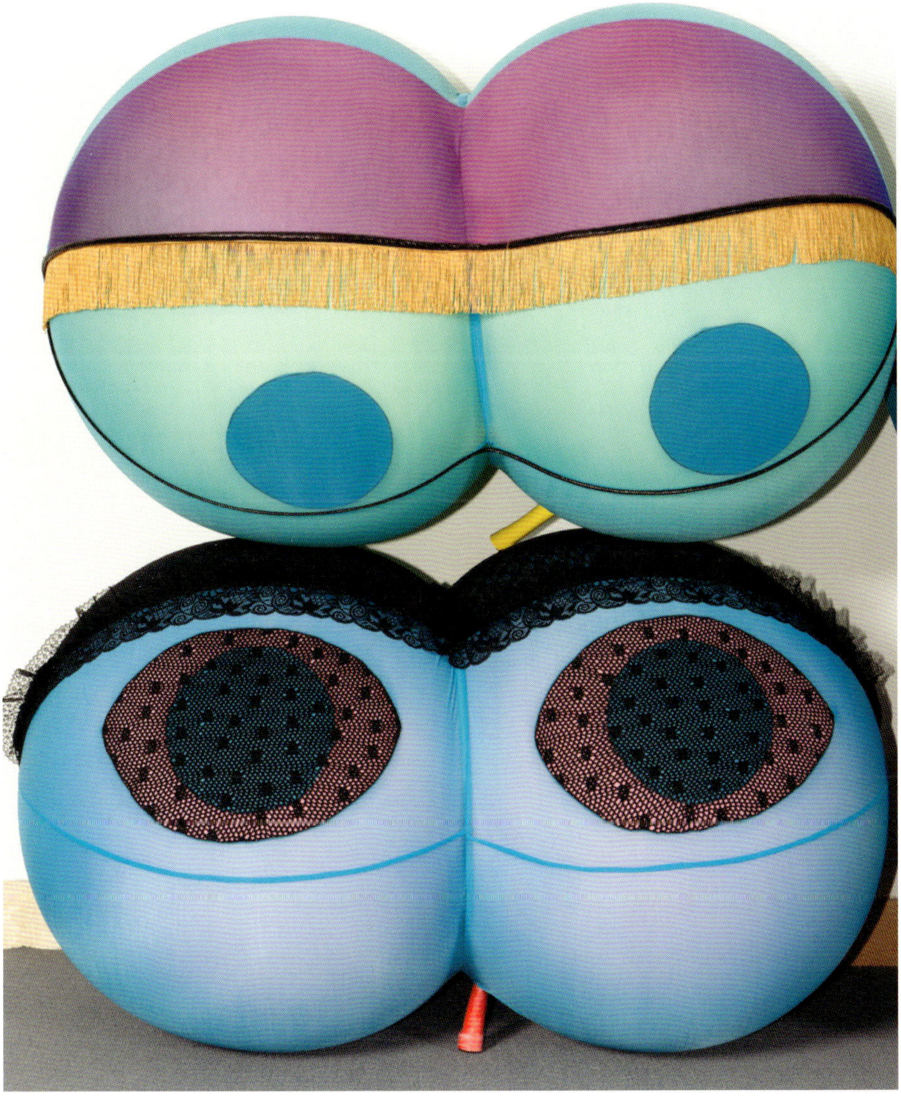

CARNIVALEYES, (1998–2005), pp 50–51, 53–55

36″ x 55″ x 34″ each
fabric, latex, rope

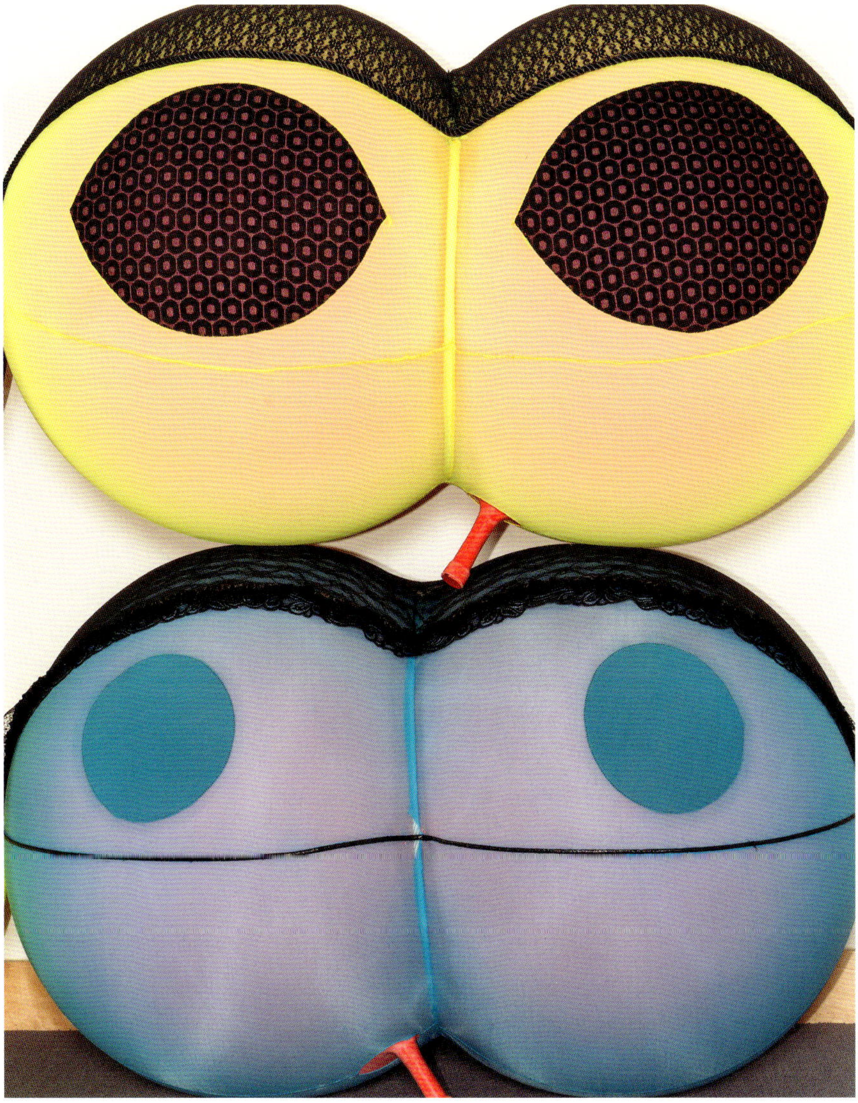

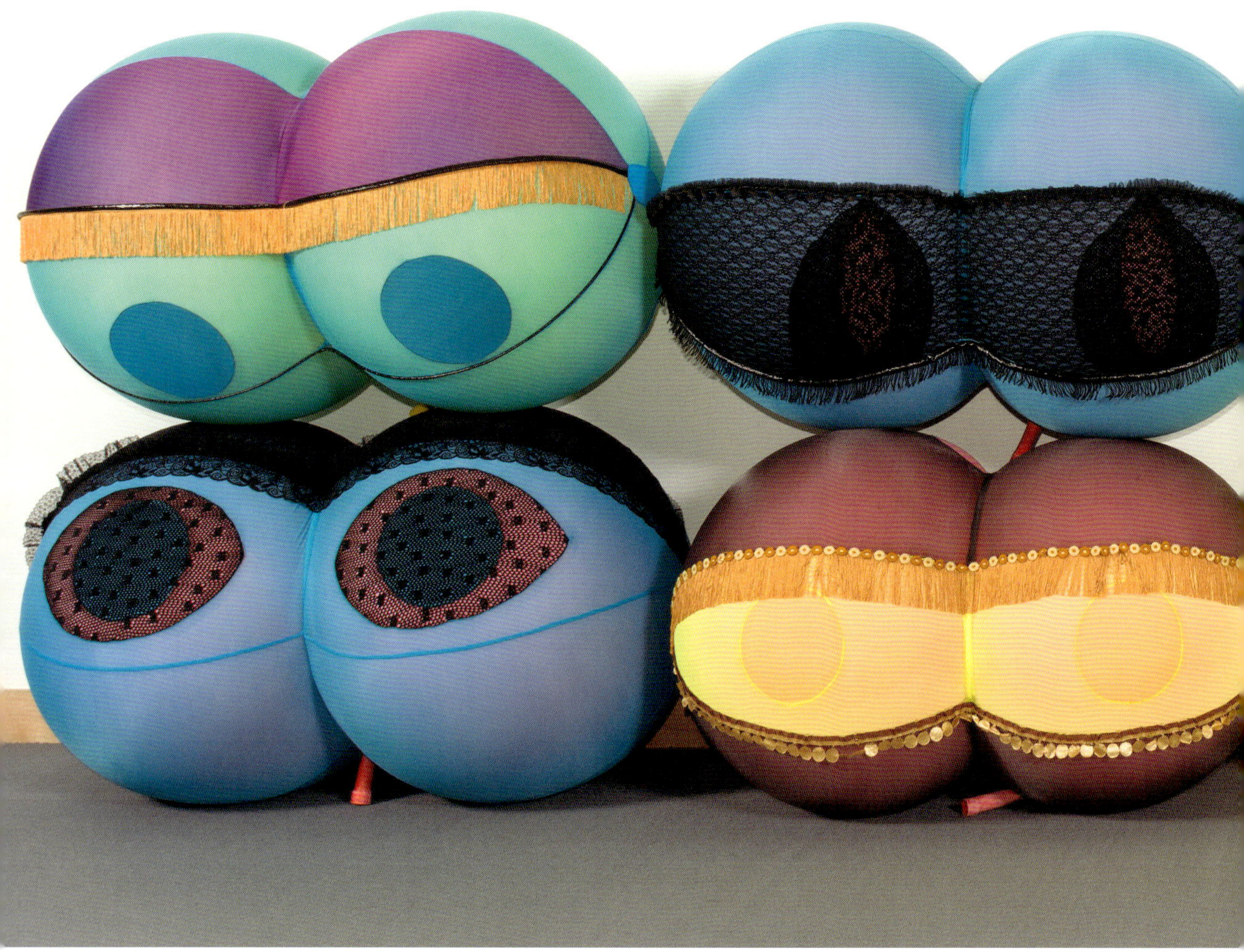

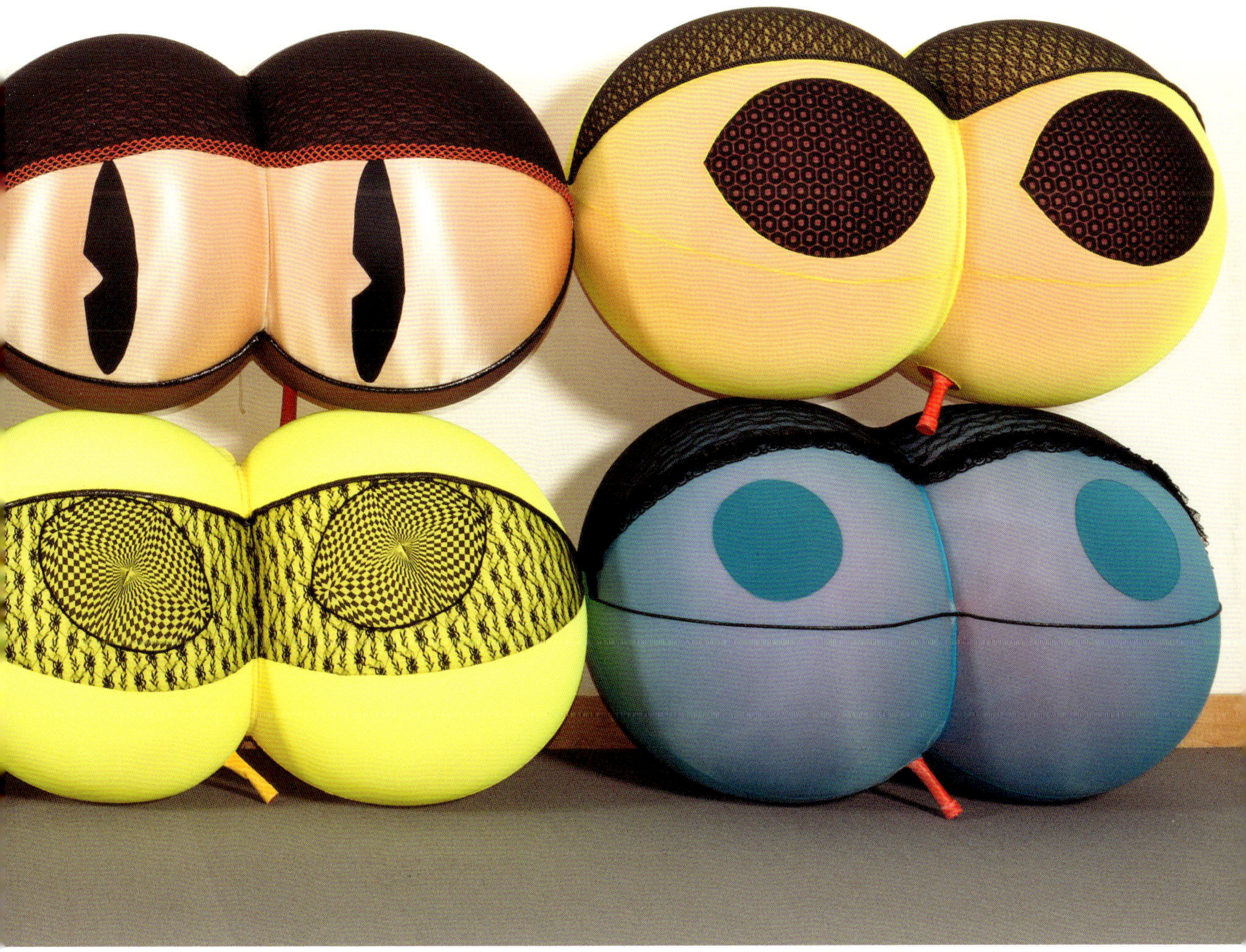

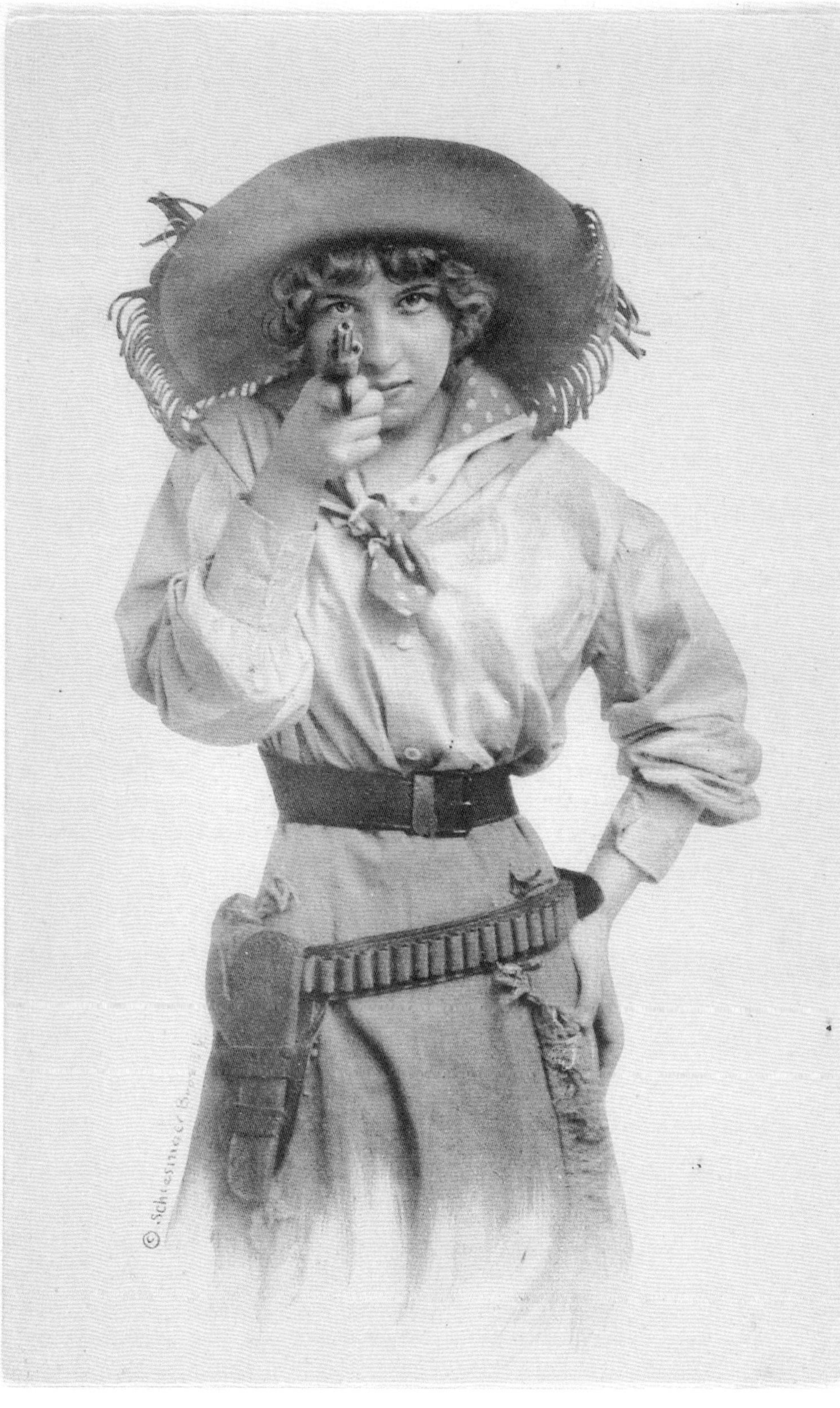

Woman wearing western clothing, 1915, Autry National Center

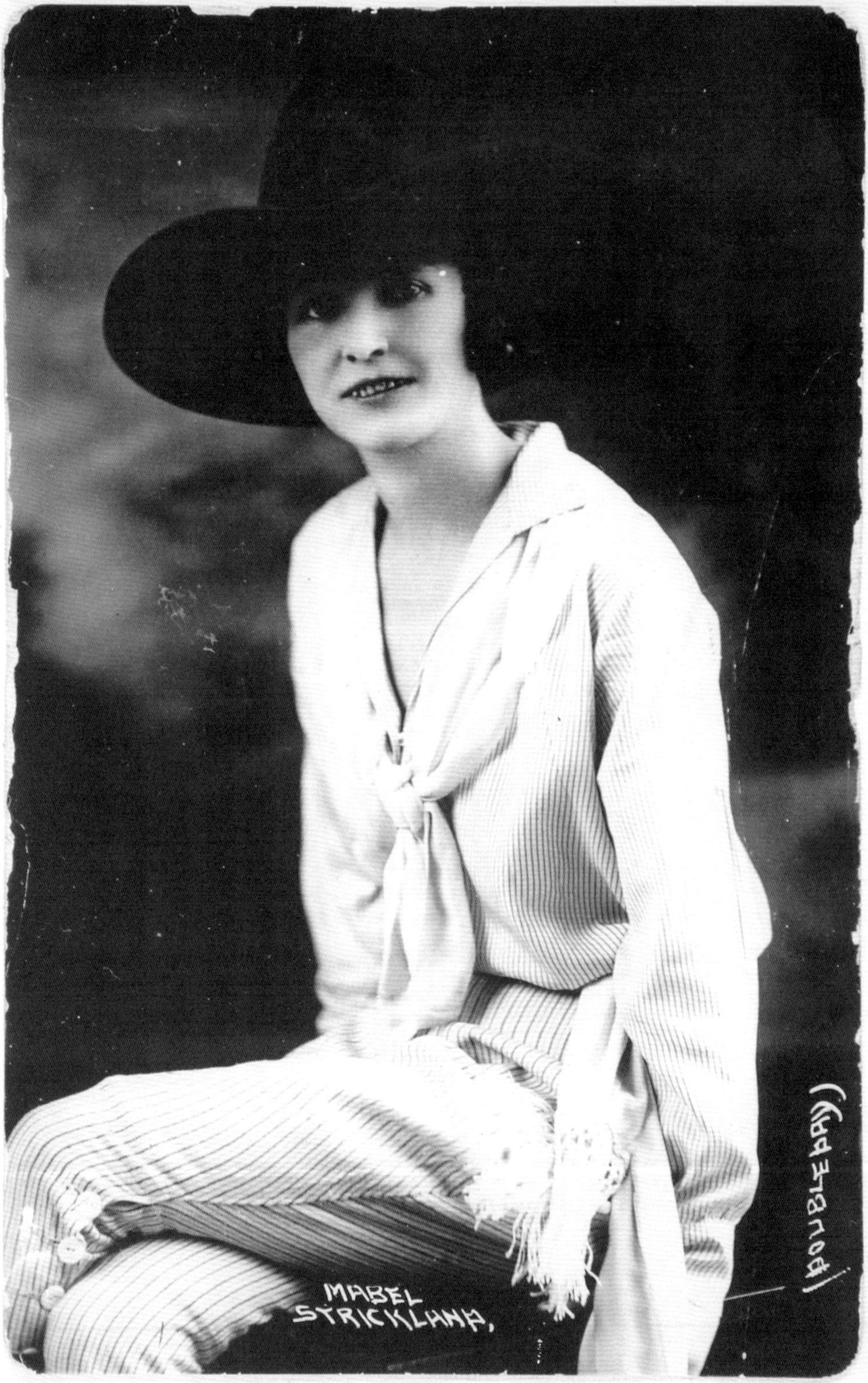

Mabel Strickland, Doubleday, 1915, Autry National Center

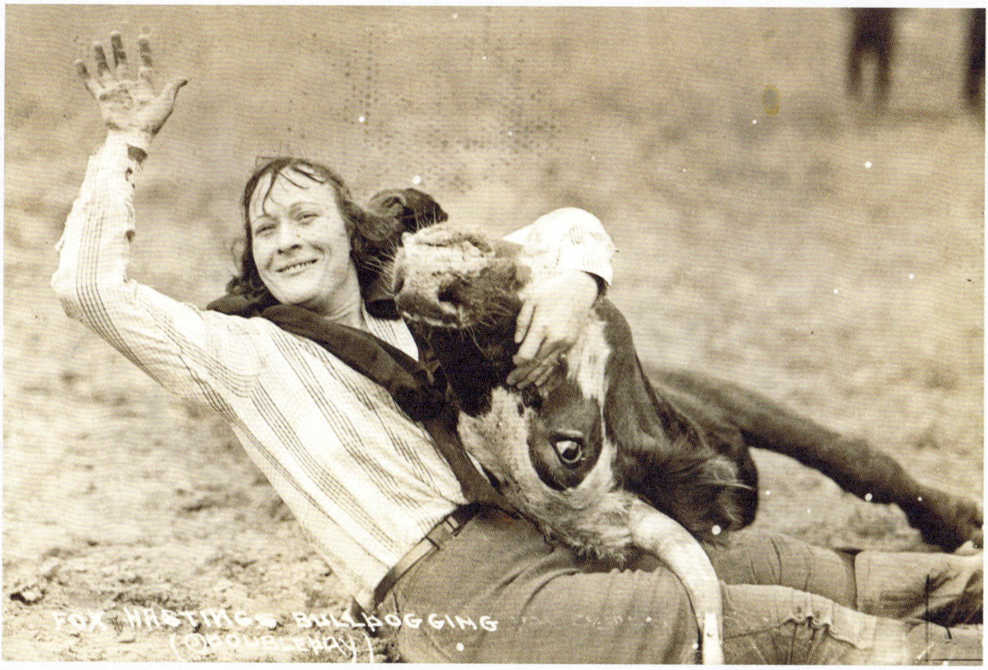

Fox Hastings bulldogging, Doubleday, Dickinson Research Center

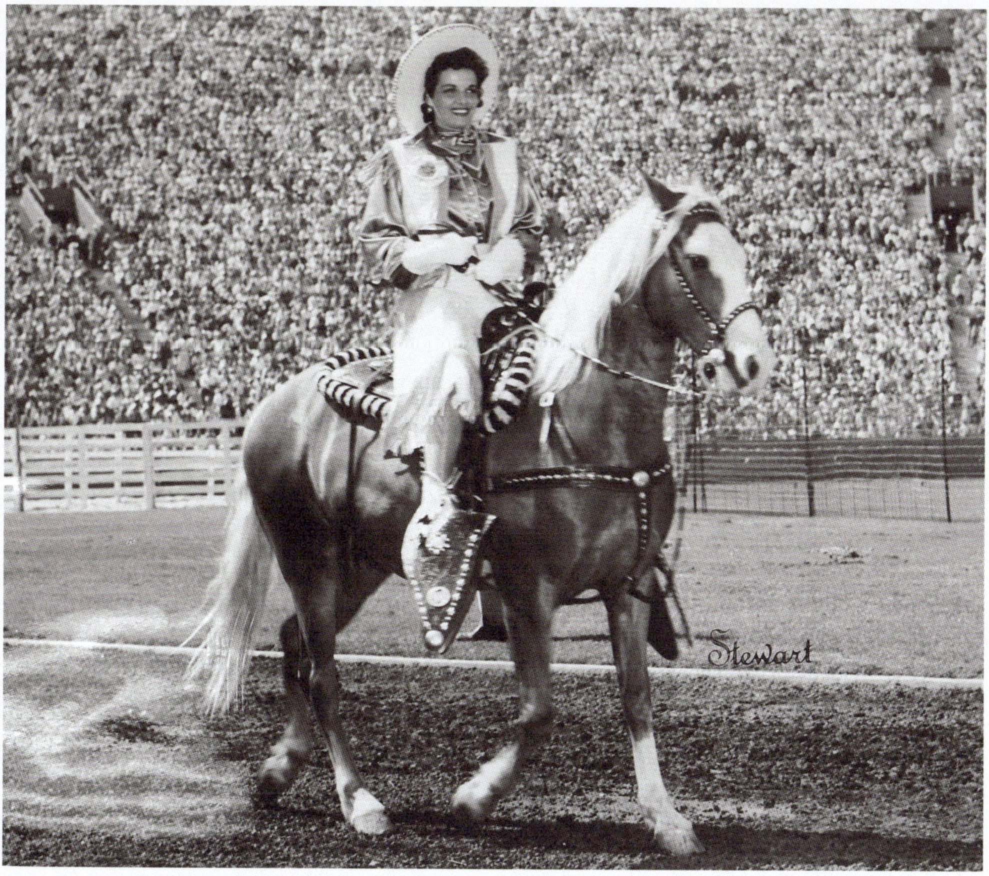

Jane Russell, Sheriff's Show, Los Angeles Coliseum, Stewart, 1949, Autry National Center

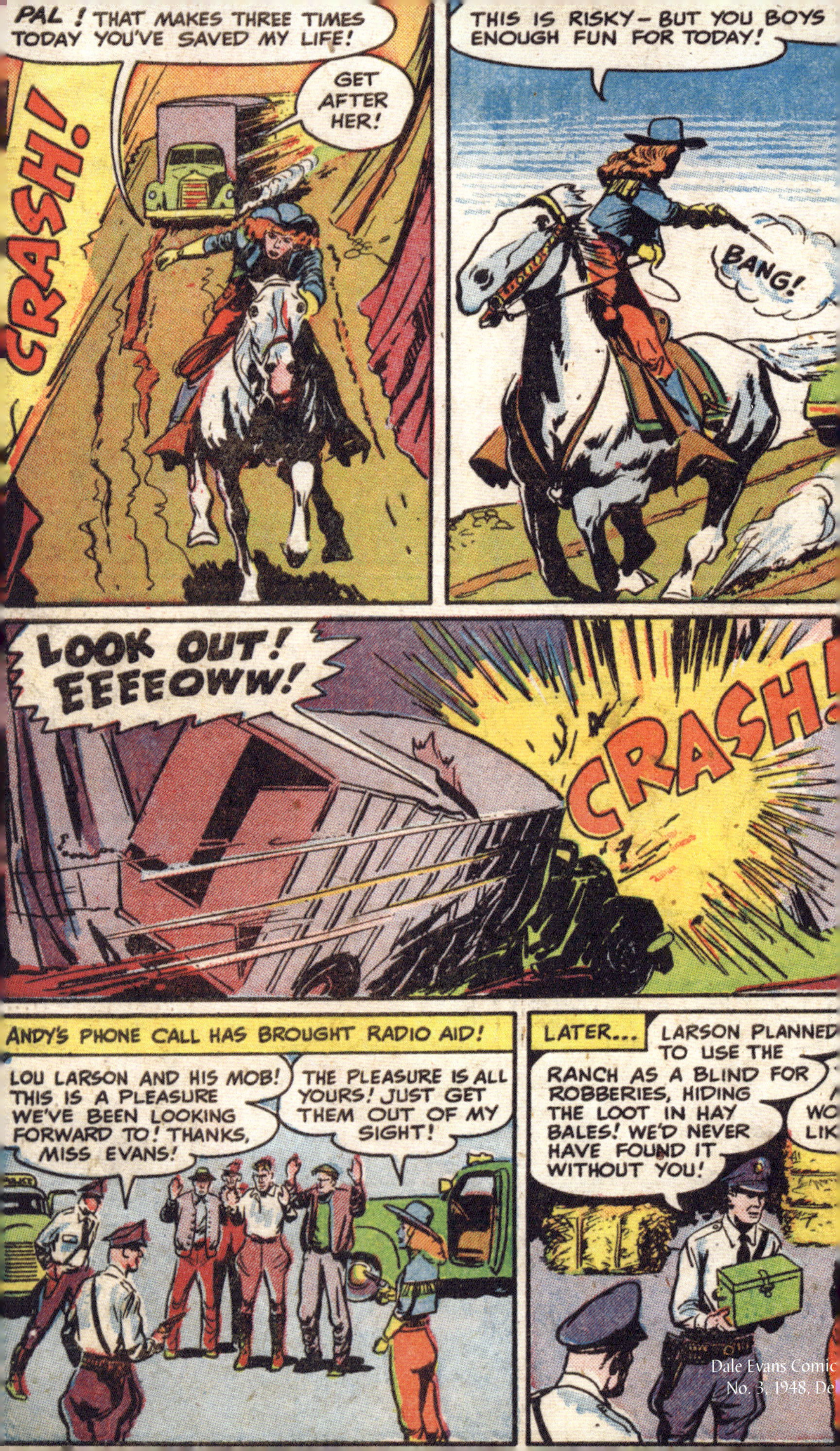

PAL! THAT MAKES THREE TIMES TODAY YOU'VE SAVED MY LIFE!
GET AFTER HER!
CRASH!
THIS IS RISKY– BUT YOU BOYS ENOUGH FUN FOR TODAY!
BANG!
LOOK OUT! EEEEOWW!
CRASH!
ANDY'S PHONE CALL HAS BROUGHT RADIO AID!
LOU LARSON AND HIS MOB! THIS IS A PLEASURE WE'VE BEEN LOOKING FORWARD TO! THANKS, MISS EVANS!
THE PLEASURE IS ALL YOURS! JUST GET THEM OUT OF MY SIGHT!
LATER...
LARSON PLANNED TO USE THE RANCH AS A BLIND FOR ROBBERIES, HIDING THE LOOT IN HAY BALES! WE'D NEVER HAVE FOUND IT WITHOUT YOU!

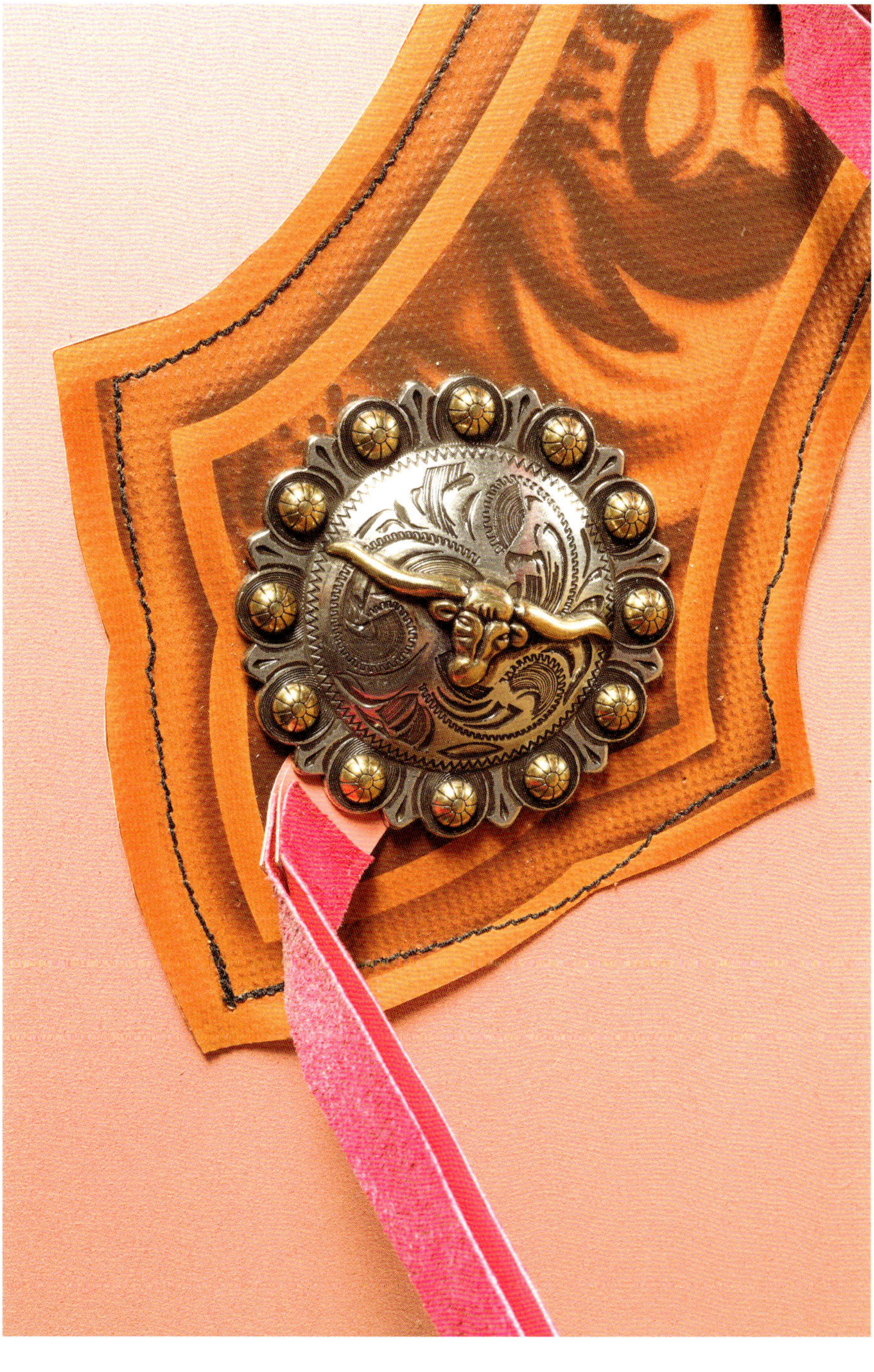

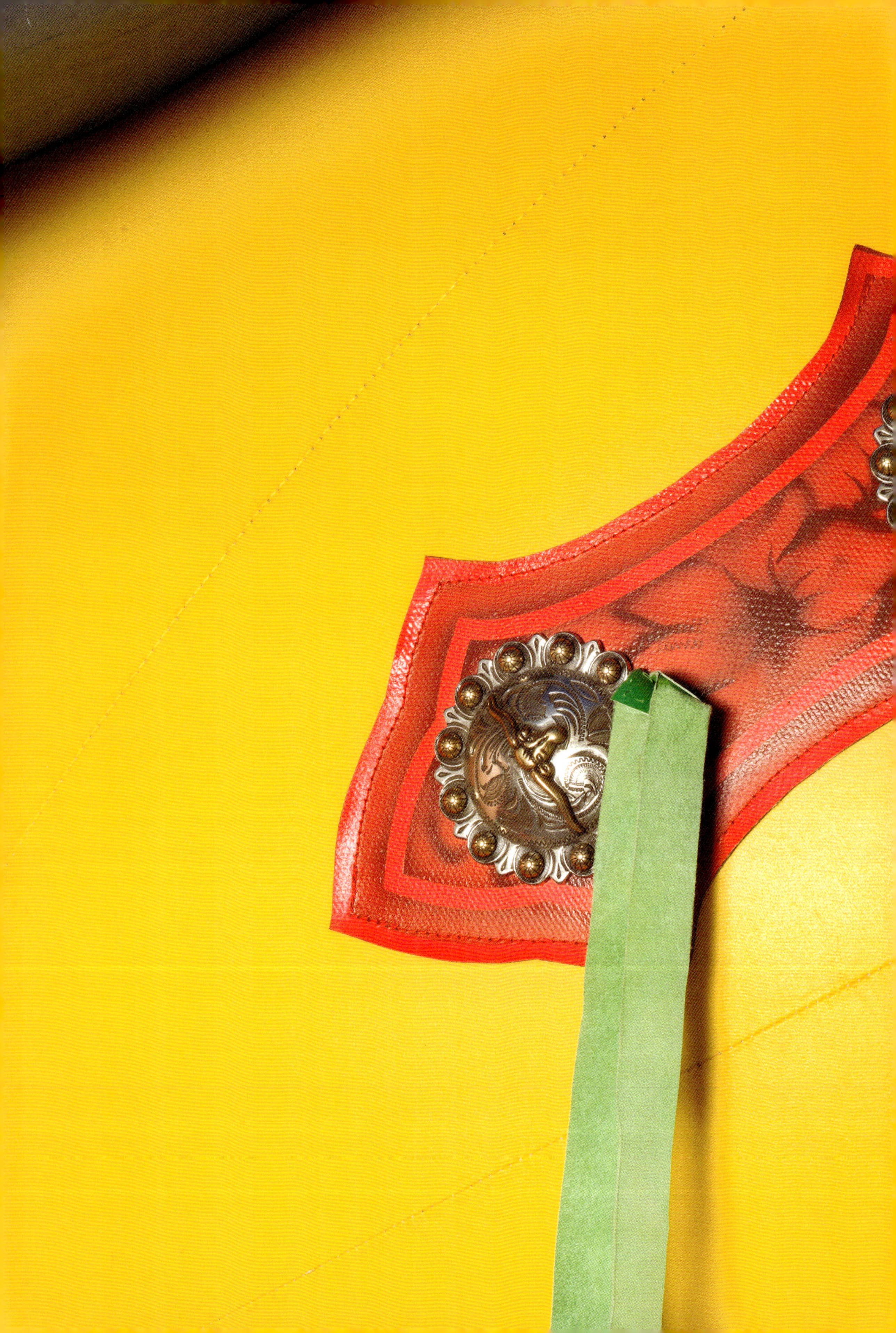

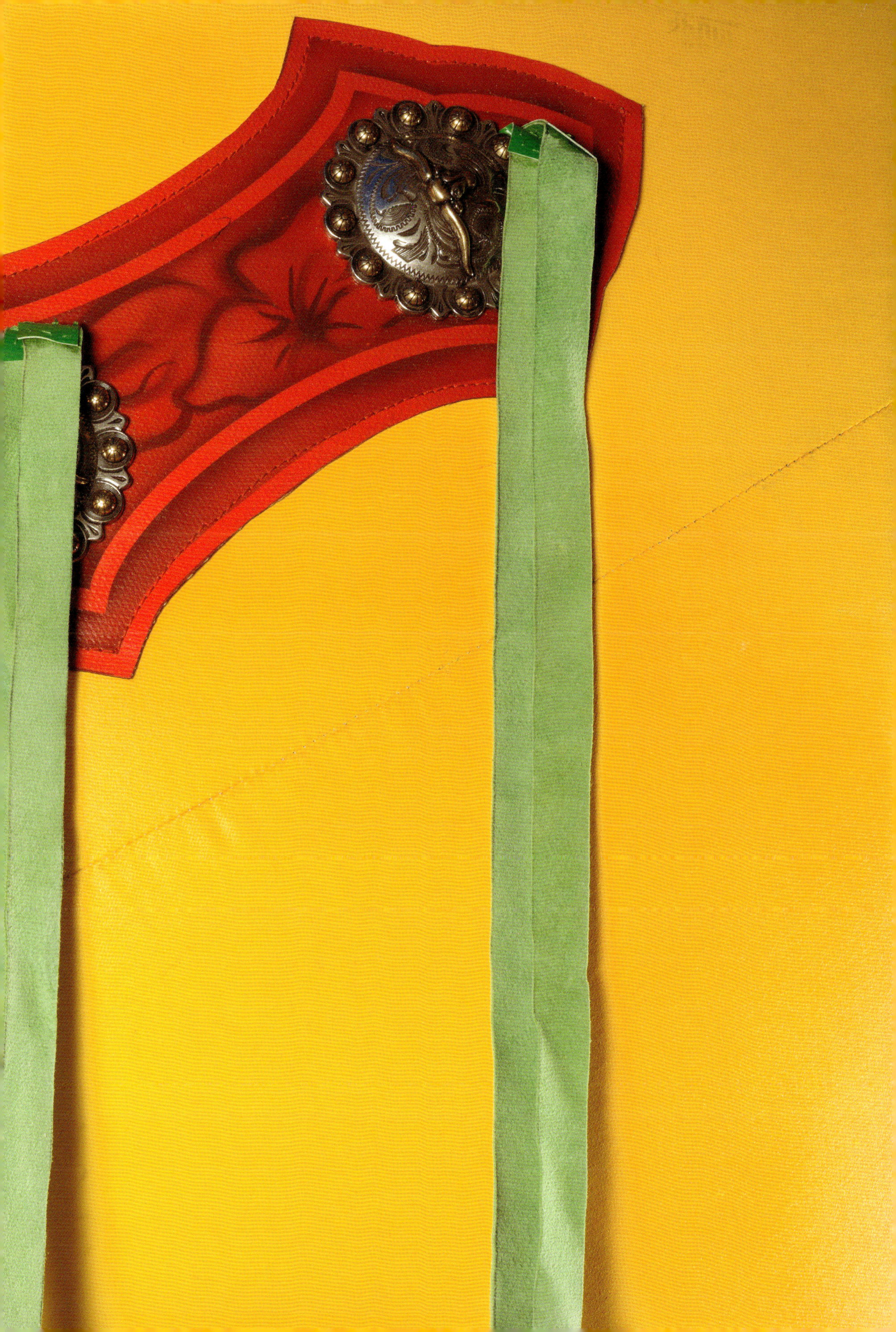

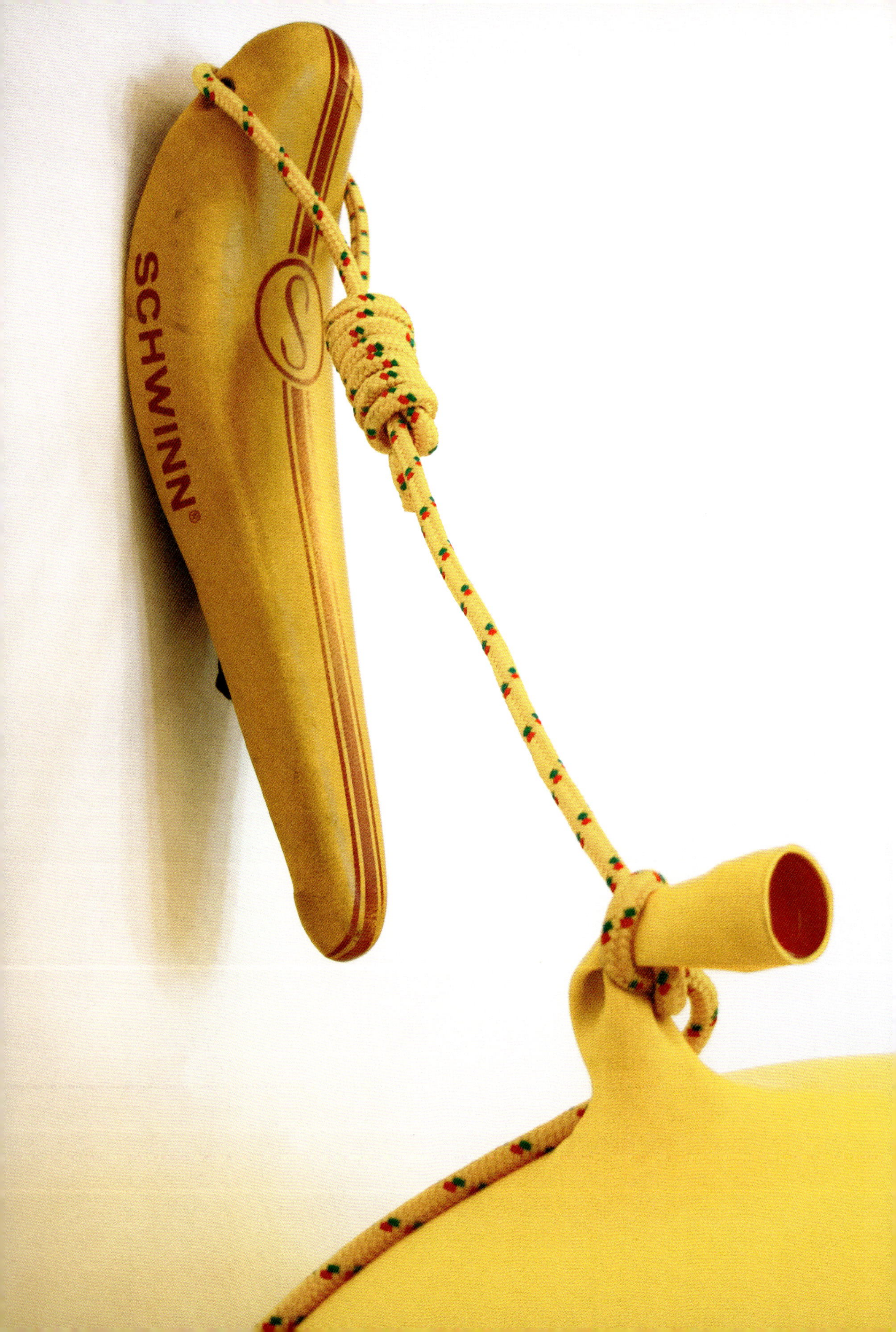
SCHWINN®

ROPED II (2013)

24" x 36"
pigment ink print

ROPED I (2013)

24" x 36"
pigment ink print

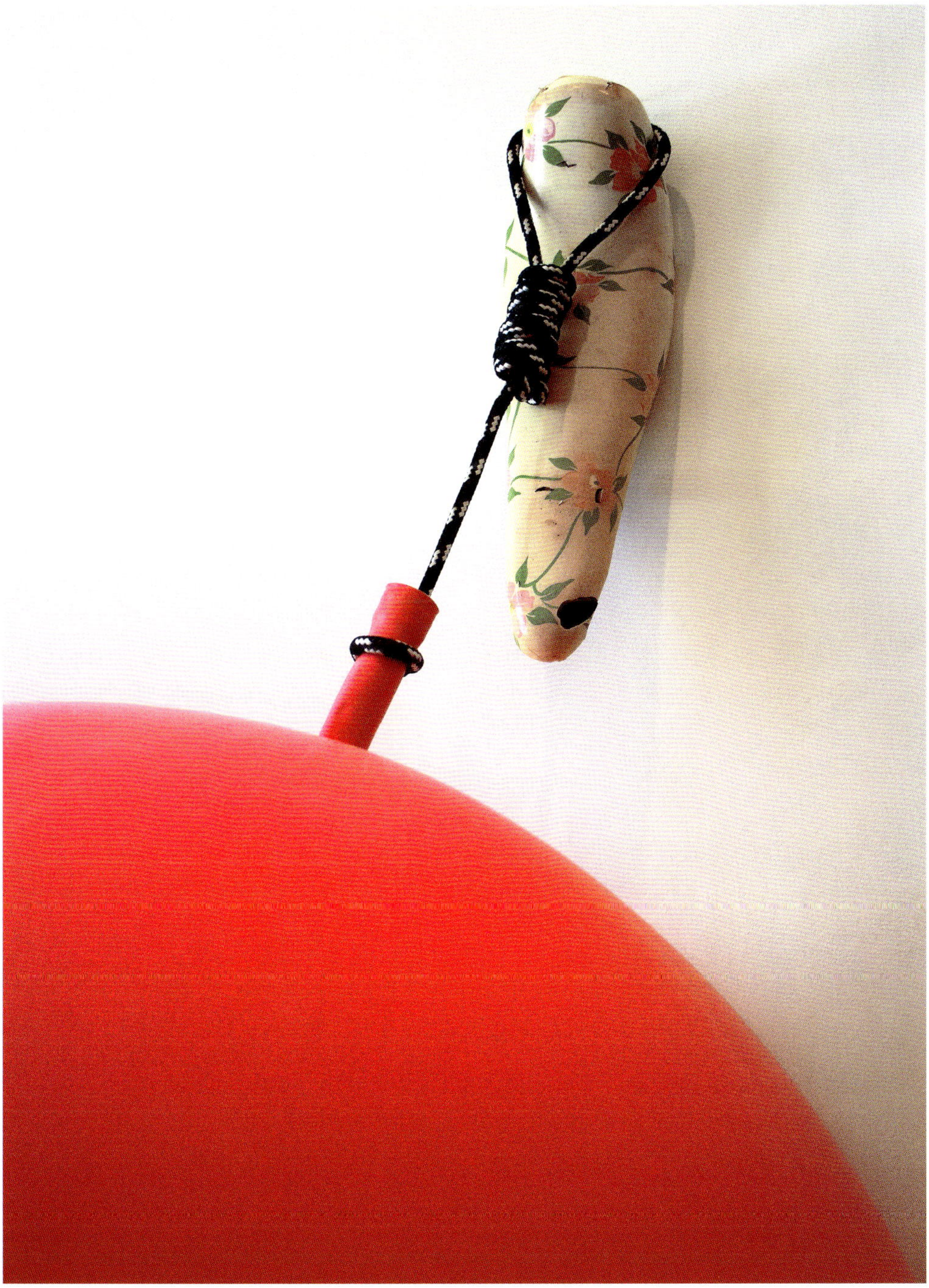

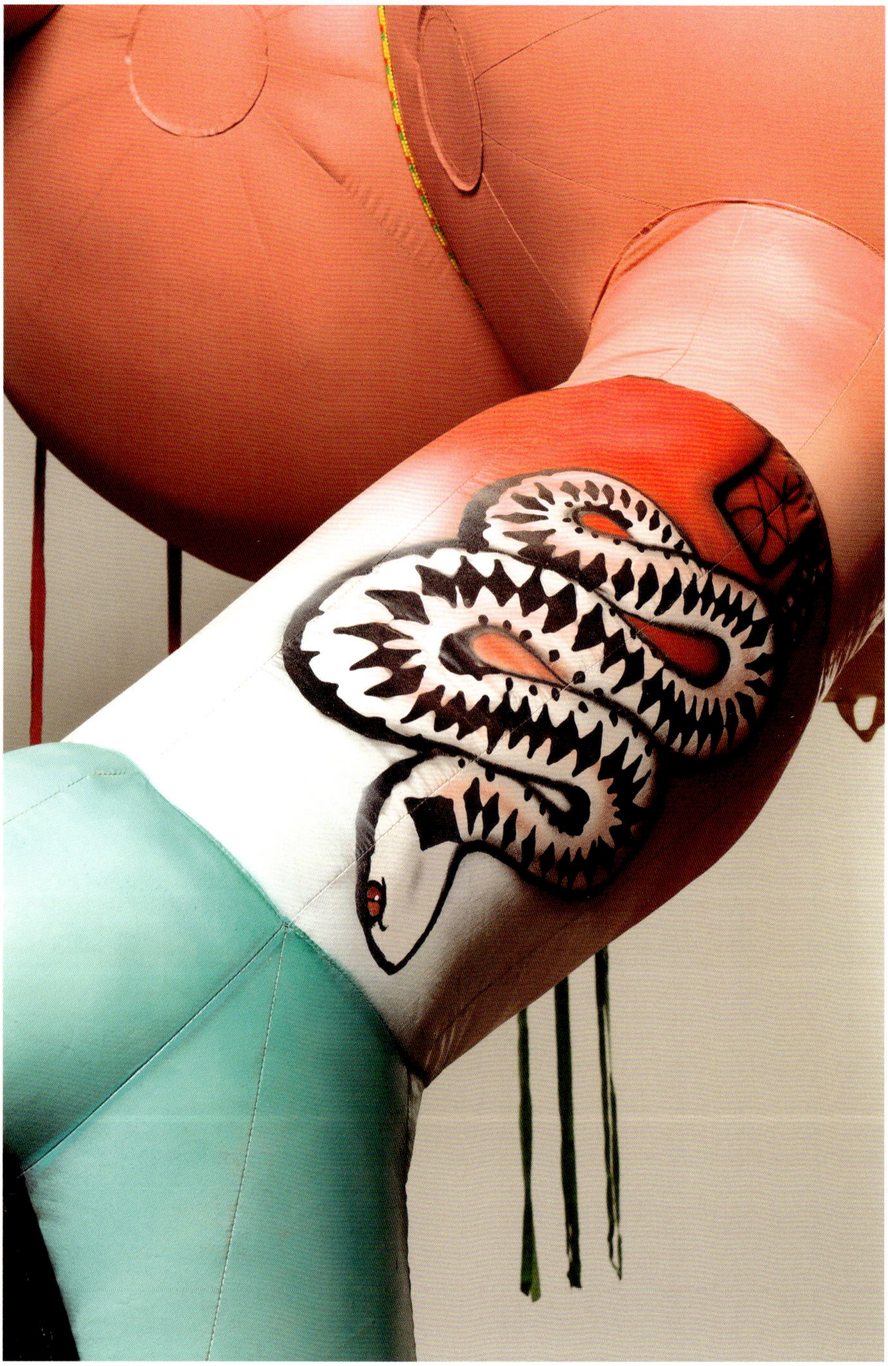

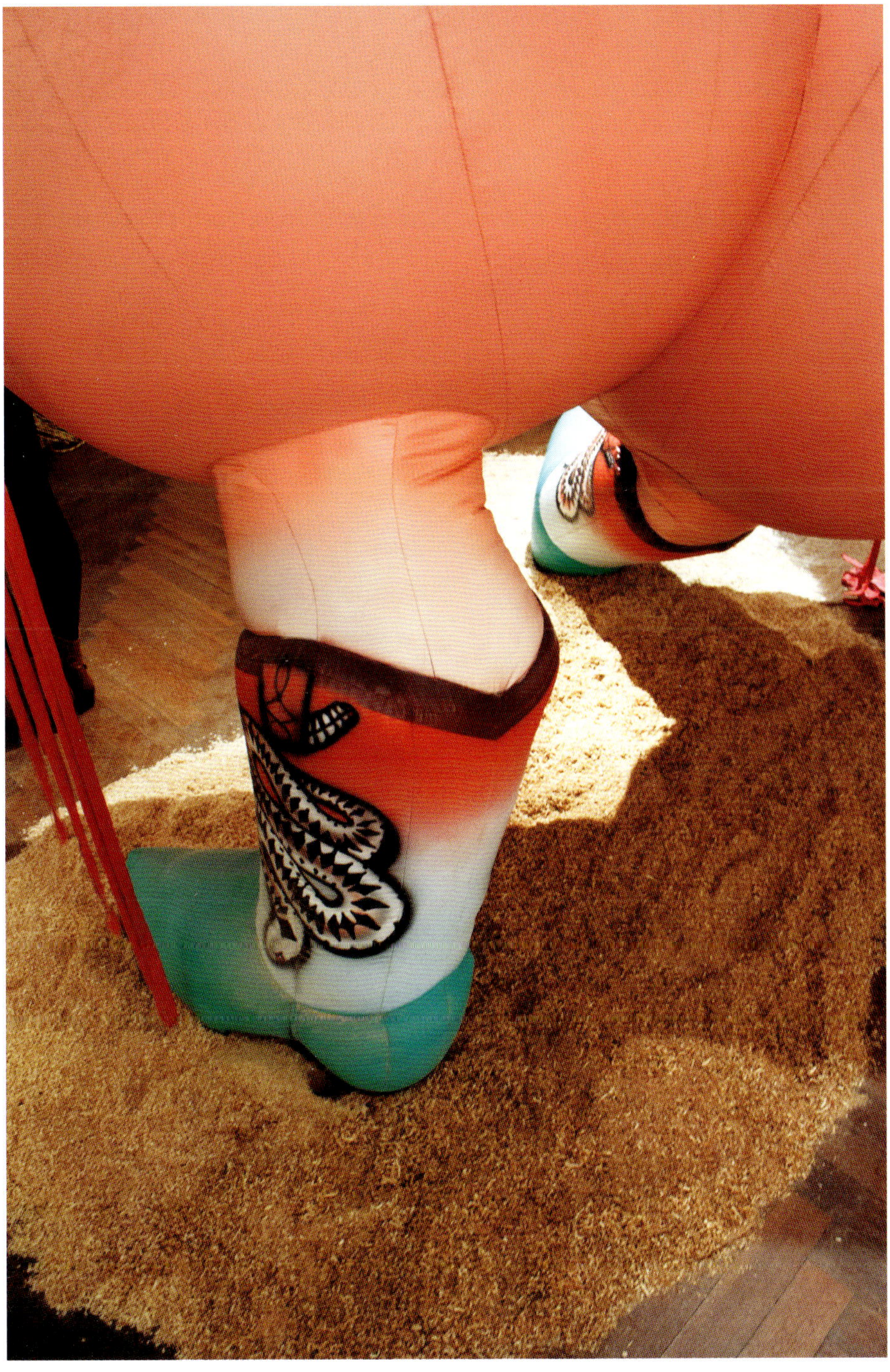

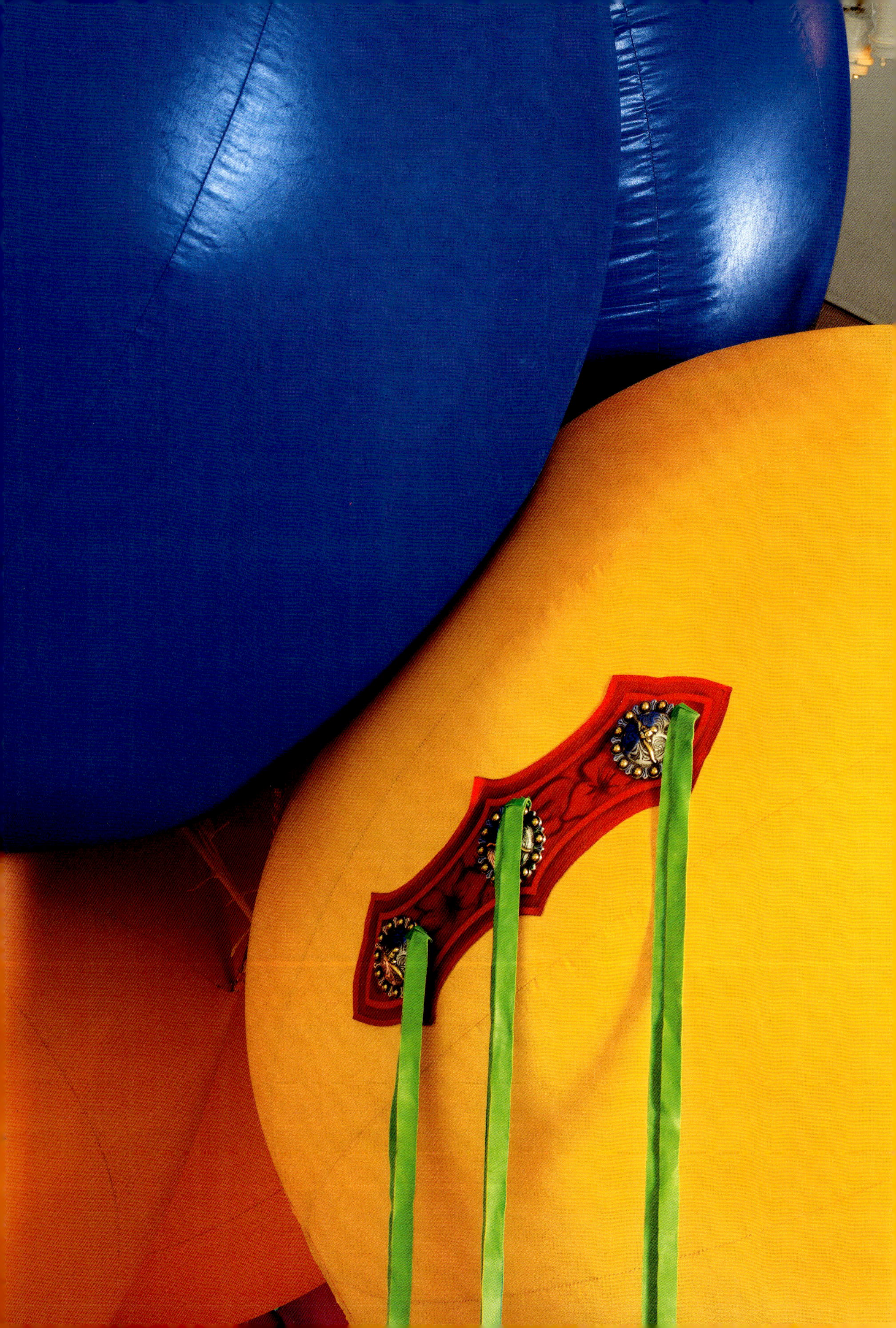

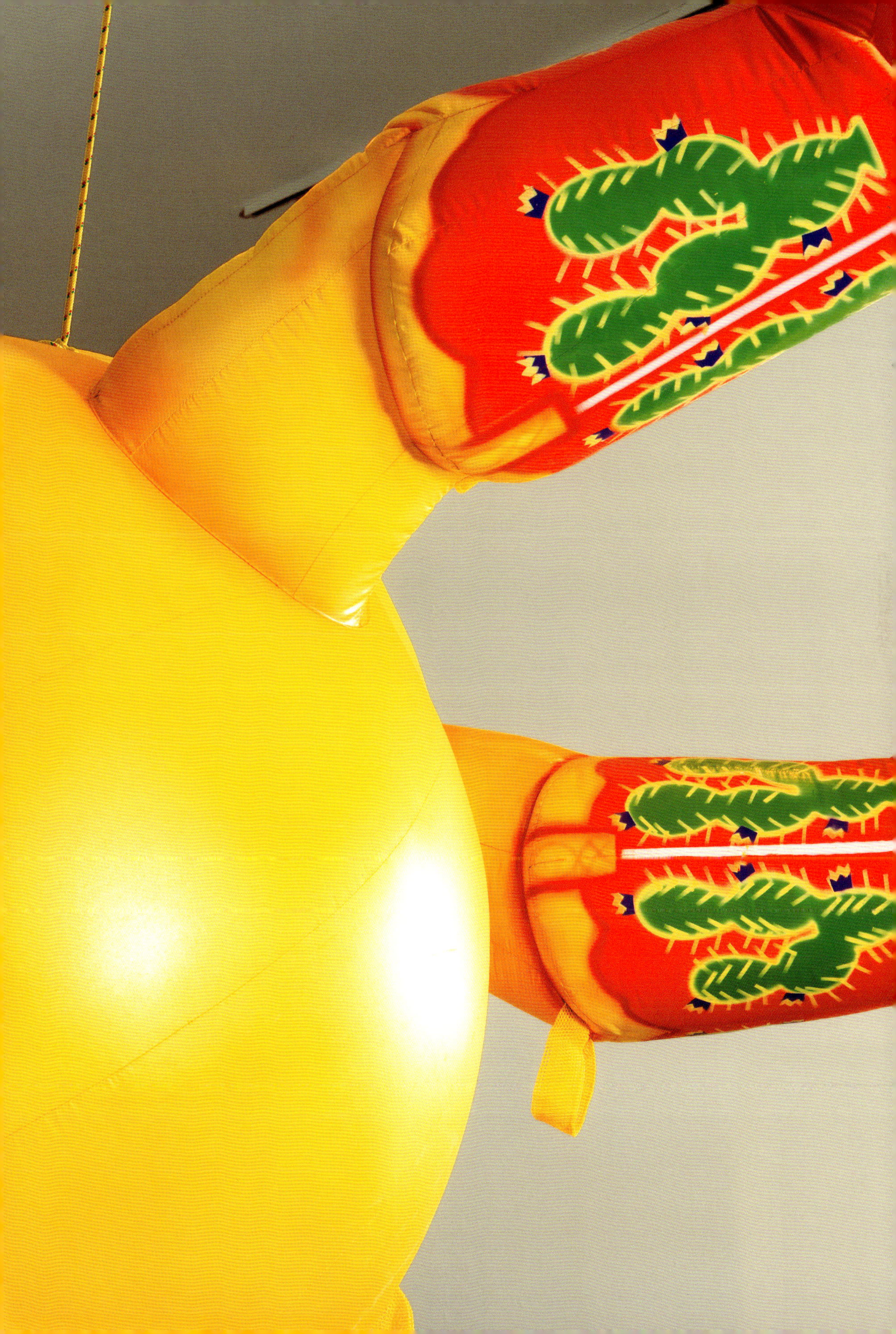

NA
DAVI

NCY
DSON

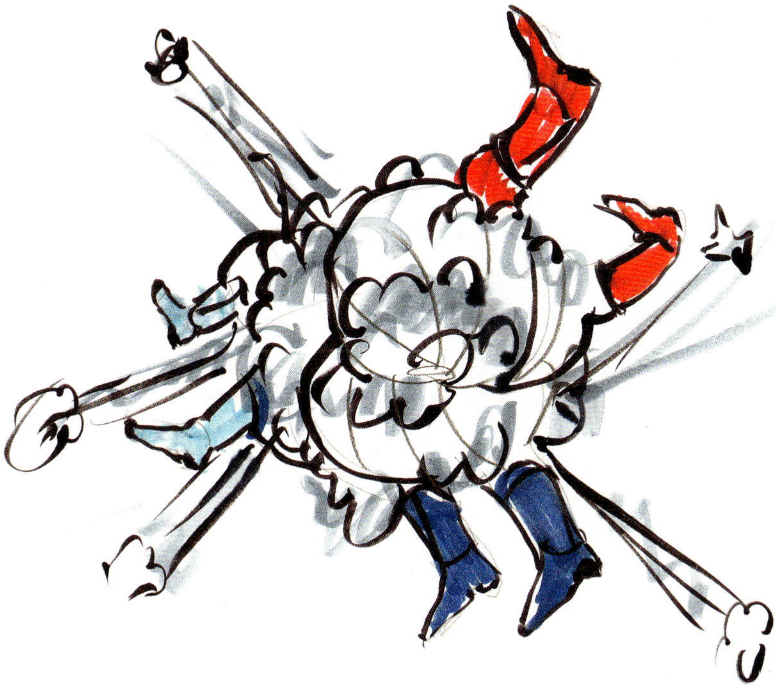

Dust up

LIKE A RHINESTONE COWGIRL: NANCY DAVIDSON'S FUNNY FEMINISM

Jessica Brier is a curator and writer living in Los Angeles. She is a doctoral student in art history at the University of Southern California and holds a BA from New York University and an MA in curatorial practice from the California College of the Arts (CCA).

Formerly a curatorial assistant in photography at the San Francisco Museum of Modern Art (SFMOMA), Brier has worked on numerous exhibitions, including Public Intimacy: Art and Other Ordinary Acts in South Africa *(2014),* South Africa in Apartheid and After: David Goldblatt, Ernest Cole, Billy Monk *(2012–13),* Jay DeFeo: A Retrospective *(2012–13), and* Francesca Woodman *(2011–12). She has written for* Art on Paper, *CCA's* Curating Now, *SFMOMA's* Open Space *blog, and Daylight Digital. She is a regular contributor to* Art Practical *and* Daily Serving. *Independently, she has organized exhibitions at the CCA Wattis Institute for Contemporary Arts; at Park Life, a gallery and store in San Francisco; and at Headlands Center for the Arts, in Sausalito, California.*

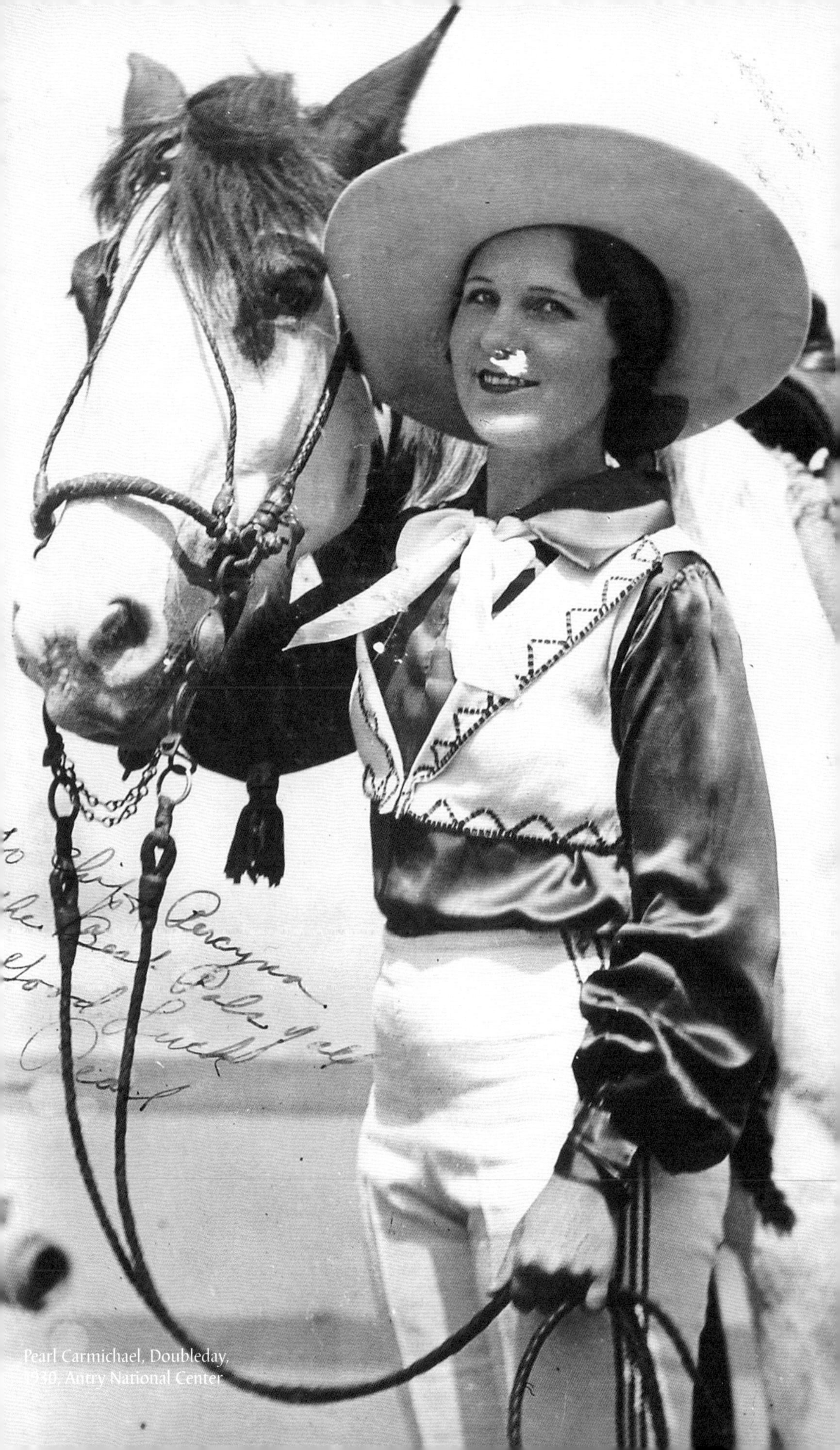

Pearl Carmichael, Doubleday, 1930, Autry National Center

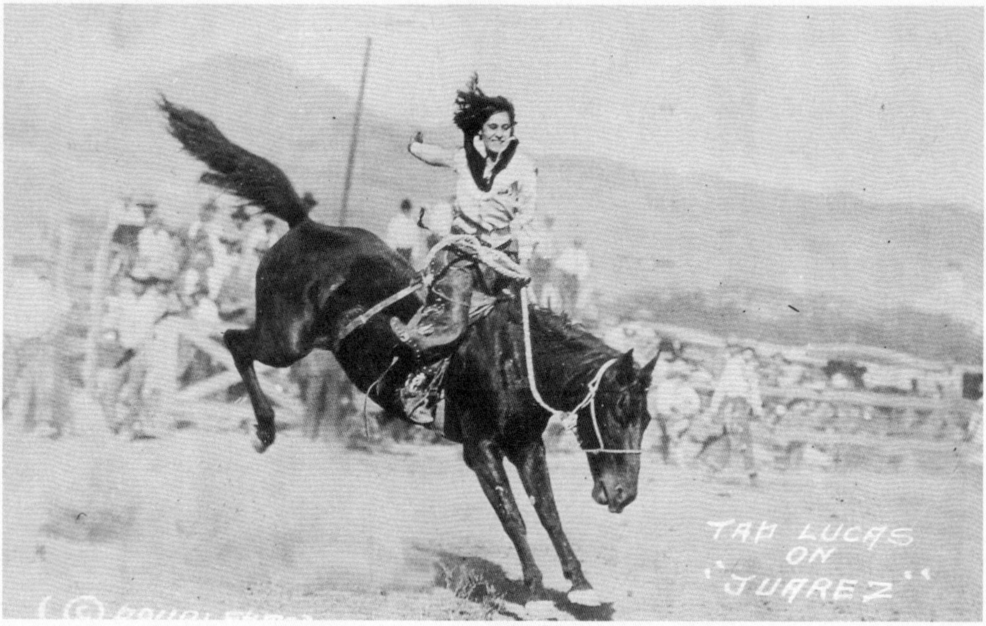

Tad Lucas on Juarez, Doubleday, 1922–1926, Autry National Center

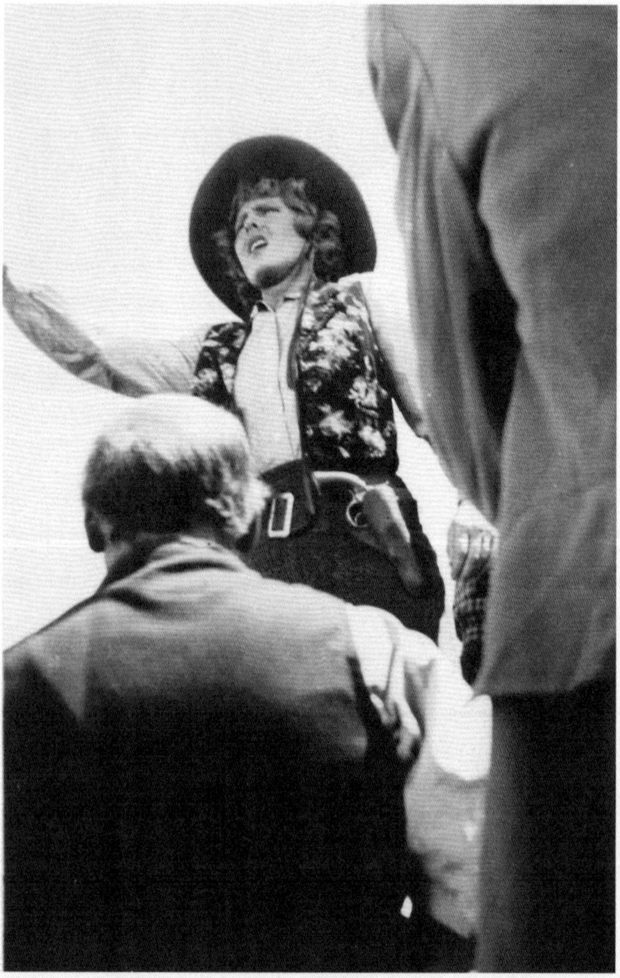

Jean Arthur in Columbia Pictures' *Arizona*, 1940, Autry National Center

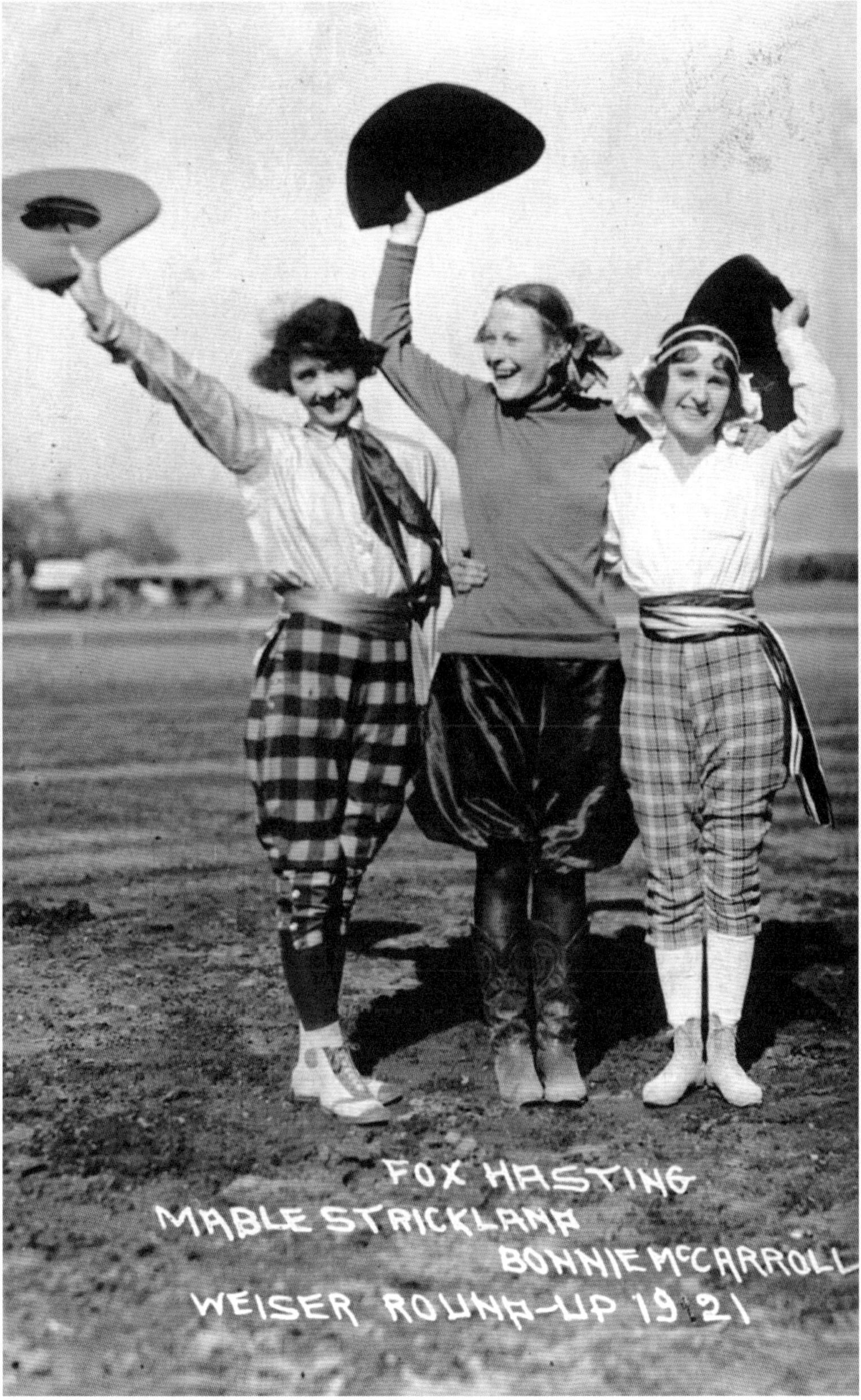

Mabel Strickland, Fox Hastings, and Bonnie McCarroll (left to right) at Weiser Round-Up, Doubleday, 1921, Dickinson Research Center

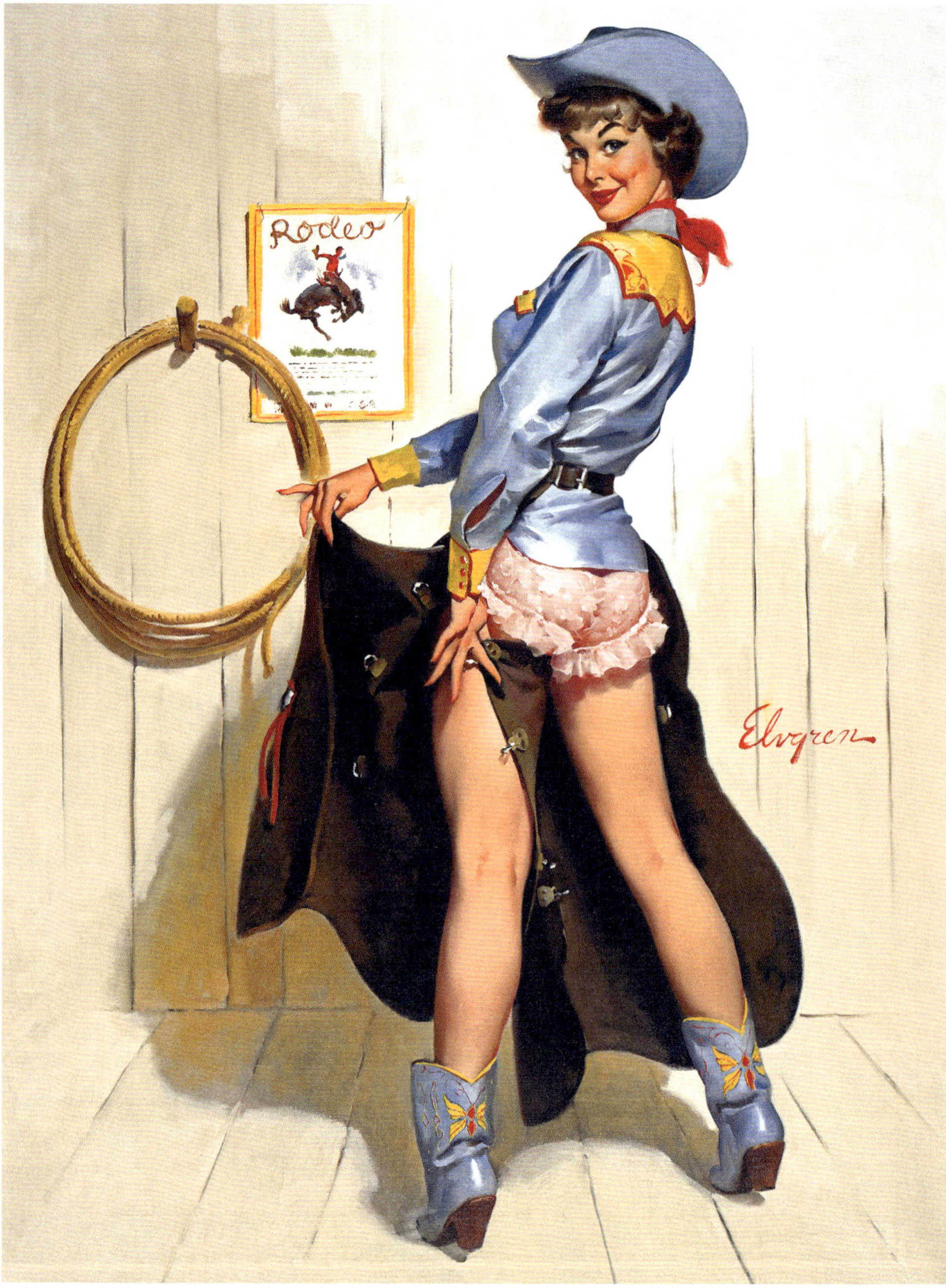

Lucky Chaps, Gil Elvgren, 1962, © Brown & Bigelow Inc., St. Paul, Minnesota *by Jessica Brier*

In 1948, the preeminent American art critic Clement Greenberg declared, in an essay called "The New Sculpture," that sculpture was on the rise and would surpass painting as the dominant modern art form. Although this dichotomy between painting and sculpture seems antiquated today, the question of whether medium specificity is meaningful or useful remains very much in play. Greenberg wrote: "And even should sculpture be compelled eventually to become as abstract as painting, it would still have a larger realm of formal possibilities at its command."[1] Nancy Davidson came of age as an artist some 25 years later, earning her MFA from the School of the Art Institute of Chicago in 1975. This was a pivotal time for many art schools, when the notion of working strictly as a painter or sculptor was starting to give way to the freedom to work fluidly among mediums. Davidson embraced this working mode right away, and fluidity is key to the complexity of the work she has made over the past four decades.[2]

The mid-'70s was also the height of the women's movement in the United States, and manifestations were evident among many women artists. As the need to stake out medium-specific territory seemed less urgent, many women began to realize how deeply gendered were the language of the art world and the commonly accepted metrics of artistic success. This confluence of artistic circumstances set the stage for Davidson's burgeoning practice, shaping the intent and reception of her work from the outset. As art historian Linda Nochlin describes it,

> a primary goal [of the women's movement in the early 1970s] was to change or displace the traditional, almost entirely male-oriented notion of "greatness" itself. There had been a particular and recent historical reconsecration of the cultural ideal of greatness in the United States in the 1950s and 1960s.[3]

The midcentury shift to which Nochlin refers is largely owed to critics like Greenberg, who upheld the association of "great" art—to use Nochlin's term—with virility, physical aggression, and machismo power, largely by glorifying abstract expressionism and its many offshoots. But even in his acclaim of sculpture, his impulse to pit one medium against another and declare a winner upholds the notion of greatness as "best," evidencing a competitive spirit that arguably kills the experimental impulse and denies the possibility that many legitimate, interesting forms of art may exist at once.

In some ways, Davidson's work reads as a very direct, female response to this attitude toward art making. However, it is worth understanding her work as different from much of what was happening in the women's movement as it manifested most visibly in art. Davidson, unlike many women artists in the 1970s, was never interested in confessional subject matter but, rather, wanted to address gender in other, perhaps less direct ways. Lynda Benglis's infamous double-page ad (which the artist referred to as a "centerfold") in the November 1974 issue of *Artforum* might be thought of as a milestone for the brand of feminism that characterized the work of artists like Davidson.[4] This iteration of the movement was one that pointed emphatically toward the centrality of sexual politics, one that acknowledged the fact of female experience as distinct without attempting to explain it. Benglis's use of fragile materials like wax in her large-scale sculptural work was of explicit interest to Davidson in the 1970s, evidencing a distinctly female approach to a working mode—namely large-scale installation—long dominated by a macho sensibility.

Davidson's practice might also be understood in the lineage of Louise Bourgeois, whose career overlapped with Davidson's but was in a later stage as Davidson found her own artistic footing. Bourgeois, deeply involved with and influenced by French surrealism, broke ground by creating art that rendered physical her own psychological state. Her work is deeply personal and even autobiographical, in a sense, very much about female experience without pointing very directly to gender itself as a subject. Bourgeois is best known for her material and spatial experiments, using form and texture to push the limits of sculpture and mining the subconscious for subject matter. Similarly, Davidson's work uses sculptural installation—the terrain of material and formal investigation—to explore physical manifestations of psychological states. The psychological made physical is, for Bourgeois and Davidson, a distinctly female pursuit—one that calls the notion of large-scale sculpture as a demonstration of "greatness" into serious question. For both artists, this is achieved largely through a particular sense of humor.

Having begun her career as an artist in Chicago, Davidson relocated to New York in 1979. In the early 1990s, she started making installations, beginning to think through issues of scale and form, deeply influenced by the work of Eva Hesse. She looked for lightweight material that could fill large spaces and discovered that she could order weather balloons through the mail. The first one to arrive at her home and studio in lower Manhattan—which, perhaps not coincidentally, sits around the corner from a balloon store—was white. She inflated it and tied the nozzle where air passes through and squeezed it into a clothing rack, immediately compelled to play with how this malleable spherical form could be manipulated. Viscerally, this material was enchanting; she was struck by the intense smell of latex emitted by the balloon and noticed how much it resembles skin when deflated. She felt that "all of life" could be read into these objects: they are buoyant and full of vitality when inflated, sad and dead when deflated, and their eventual degradation is inevitable, like the materials Hesse used. Davidson's video *Breathless* (1999) is an absurdist and durational ode to the balloon, indulging in and heightening the sensorial intensity of the materials.

Davidson's work with inflatables has become a decades-long experiment, using a material already imbued with anthropomorphic qualities to create forms that are both abstract and highly suggestive. At the heart of these works is the constant question: "Why is humor in art not taken seriously?" Her works employ Freudian connotations of the most basic forms—nodding directly to Bourgeois—using volume, color, and texture. Two pink, round spheres pushed together and bound by rope or draped with what looks like the lacy hem of the skirt become bawdy suggestions of a buxom female anatomy. These forms connote and question ideals of beauty and expectations of female sexuality with cunning subtlety and humor, masquerading as simple, ridiculously cartoonish, colorful forms. *Buttress* (1997), a stack of hot pink latex balloons clad in shiny silver fabric, is both a towering, abstract sculptural form and a clear reference to progressively skimpy underwear on a parade of disembodied rear ends, unmistakably suggested by its title.

The more one looks at these works, the more their inherent contradictions become clear: these ebullient, seemingly easy forms are results of insistent, almost violent manipulation of materials. They are aggressively squeezed, tied, and bound together, often existing in a delicate physical state of equilibrium. Suggestions of bondage are brought to mind as anthropomorphic forms become visible in works such as

Maebe (1997), a relatively early sculptural work made of latex balloon, net, fabric, plaster, and rope that sends up and pays tribute to classic Hollywood sex symbol Mae West. Davidson acknowledges that physical control is an important aspect of her artistic process, no doubt related to the complexity of sexuality (particularly of women) that is at the center of much of the work.

Davidson's work is laden with cultural and literary references. One of Davidson's favorite novels is Jeanette Winterson's *Sexing the Cherry* (1989), a magical realist tale of the Dog-Woman, a giant, grotesque figure, and her son in 17th-century London. The Dog-Woman character resonates with Davidson's interest in "roadside giants," Americana kitsch monuments that loom alongside highways advertising diners and truck stops. Roadside giants are typically gendered to a comical degree, taking the form of Paul Bunyan as a man or Marilyn Monroe as a woman. Winterson's novel offered a potent foil to these images and became a touchstone for Davidson's interest in using scale to address and complicate gender. Davidson cites the writings of Winterson, Susan Stewart, Mary Russo, and Mikhail Bakhtin as "the intellectual underpinnings of my fascination with gigantic, grotesque, erotic, absurd, comic characters." Bakhtin's theories of the carnivalesque and grotesque, tracing the way carnivals upend social order and throw power dynamics out of whack by means of humor and chaos, foreground Davidson's use of humor as a destabilizing force. Experiences like the carnival, which exists outside the normal social order and therefore operates under a wildly different set of rules, are exactly what Davidson strives to create as an artist. She likens her artistic position to that of the fool, or Shakespearean jester, who inserts herself into a situation just long enough to set mayhem in motion, then steps back to let natural social forces take their course.

Davidson began by working primarily in the visual language of abstraction and eventually moved away from it—or, more precisely, began to play with the tension between abstraction and figuration—in what she describes as an effort to "reach toward" viewers. Audience engagement has long been a primary concern for Davidson, and her interest in popular culture both informs and springs from this awareness. Walking the line between abstraction and figuration through material experimentation has, for Davidson, been a way of complicating the cultural dichotomy between high- and lowbrow. Davidson brings to her work a fascination with the theatrical and absurdist qualities of favorite American pastimes, such as the Macy's Thanksgiving Day Parade, Halloween, Mardi Gras, and other modern iterations of Bakhtin's carnival. Her work simultaneously celebrates and satirizes popular culture, always looking critically at familiar images that bring people pleasure and reinforce social control and hegemonic values, ultimately calling social order radically into question. A central example is the American cowgirl—an image, fantasy, and actual identity all at once—to which Davidson's body of work *Let 'er Buck* is dedicated. Interestingly, this point of inspiration began to surface on September 11, 2001, when Davidson found herself watching the World Trade Center collapse from her apartment window. This experience triggered emotions about Davidson's past and her complicated identity as an American. The cowgirl, an image and idea potent in its associations with 1950s popular culture and also with female empowerment, emerged as a personal guide through the devastating tragedy. Cowgirl culture is distinctly American, tied to regional history and tradition, but is also a symbol of sexual liberation (or at least a diversified idea of womanhood) and a vessel for the projection of a multitude of female tropes. This subject is a way for Davidson to reconcile her own feelings about being American—a position that incites both celebration and critique.

Figures like Dale Evans, who was feminine, sweet, and always loyal to her longtime costar and husband, Roy Rogers, loomed large in the 1950s and early 1960s, on the heels of World War II and amidst the Cold War, in an America desperate for comfort, stability, and wholesome fun. Hopes and fantasies of femininity and heteronormativity were projected onto the all American Evans. But the cowgirl was a classic symbol of surreptitious dissent for many women throughout the 20th century. While a popular image was upheld on television and in Hollywood, simultaneously there was a countercultural image—and reality—of cowgirls as androgynous, physically tough and intimidating, and distinctly unfeminine. Even in popular culture, the cowgirl was a multifaceted trope. Like the legendary cowgirl Annie Oakley, Evans was stylish, feminine, and traditionally beautiful but at the same time hardy, physically capable, and possessed of traditionally male skills.

Davidson's installation *Dustup* (2012) incorporates vinyl-coated nylon, rope, leather, blowers, sawdust, and sandbags, mimicking the shape of a comic dustball, a form that appears in cartoons or comics to indicate extreme speed or chaos, as in a chase between Wile E. Coyote and Road Runner, or Bugs Bunny and Elmer Fudd. Suspended in midair, the work is over the top in tone, color palette, and scale, somehow simultaneously cartoonish and imbued with pent-up sexual energy. Like the Macy's parade of the late 1920s or like Halloween in its original iteration, the work is expressive, pleasurable, and unmistakably dark all at once. *RowdyAnn* (2012)—a slumping wall sculpture made of fabric, foam, wood, plastic, and metal—abstracts the human body, morphing it into cowgirl props and costume, like a woman's feet deformed by too many years of wearing too-high heels.

Imposing but docile, these sculptural works hold some of the same contradictions and paradoxes as the image of the cowgirl: They are fierce and intimidating but at the same time passive and deferential. They are domineering and highly sexualized, comically flirting with the viewer with a wink and a nod, but also genuinely erotic. They take Robert Rauschenberg's "combine"—his term for an artwork that married properties of painting and sculpture—to a new and, arguably, distinctly female place. They meld together unlikely materials, images (both original and found), tropes, characters, and lived experience. They are amalgamations of emotion, passion, and humor manifest through visual and material exploration. The cowgirl, as subject, and womanhood by extension, are satirized, celebrated, and critiqued.

In her recent book, *Our Aesthetic Categories: Zany, Cute, Interesting*, literary scholar and theorist Sianne Ngai calls for the addition of "zany," "cute," and "interesting" to the canon of understood aesthetic categories used to describe literature and art.[5] Her terms are posed in direct response to specific works of contemporary art, as an alternative to imposing outdated theoretical language on artwork that operates in new ways. I propose the addition of "funny," which is certainly related to and often encompasses Ngai's terms, as an aesthetic term to help understand contemporary art.

It is important to think of humor as an artistic tool, akin to formal abstraction and use of materials, in understanding Davidson's work. Davidson seeks to create an audience experience more like that of a carnival than the relatively passive act of visiting a gallery or museum. The physically imposing nature of the work forces participatory reception; it gets in the way and insists on a physical encounter. This participation directly relates to the effects of humor on a viewer or audience: laughter is an uncontrolled, visceral, and bodily reaction, one that is emotional and physical. It affects our bodies and can take us completely by surprise. Large-scale sculptural installation is also a shared experience, one that turns individual viewers into a collective audience, thereby creating an exchange between audience members and also between audience and artist. As Davidson describes it,

> the work is engaged with spectatorship and the interaction, reaction, and attention to an implied social structure that sets up an almost irrepressible release of laughter.... I'm interested in the subversive potential of humor. It catches you from behind: "What am I laughing at? Why am I finding this pleasurable? Is this offensive?"[6]

Part of this subversion is at the crux of humor itself: the conflation of pleasure and discomfort, the sense of being both in control of and wrong-footed by one's own reaction to an image or experience. Davidson puts it simply: "Laughter is uncontrollable and unruly."

NOTES

1. Clement Greenberg, "The New Sculpture," *Art and Culture: Critical Essays* (Beacon Press, 1961).
2. In 1974, Davidson began making what she calls "installation drawings," rubbings on strips of paper made on the floor and installed systematically. (Email and notes from Nancy Davidson to the author, December 27, 2013.)
3. Linda Nochlin, "'Why Have There Been No Great Women Artists?' Thirty Years Later," *Women Artists at the Millenium*, Carol Armstrong and Catherine de Zegher, eds. (MIT Press/October Books, 2006).
4. Roberta Smith, "Art or Ad or What? It Caused a Lot of Fuss," *New York Times*, July 24, 2009, http://www.nytimes.com/2009/07/25/arts/design/25benglis.html?_r=0.
5. Sianne Ngai, *Our Aesthetic Categories: Zany, Cute, Interesting* (Harvard University Press, 2012).
6. Kate Gilmore, "Nancy Davidson with Kate Gilmore," *Brooklyn Rail*, September 3, 2012, http://www.brooklynrail.org/2012/09/art/nancy-davidson-with-kate-gilmore.

A CONVERSATION

Kate Gilmore works in multiple media, including video, sculpture, photography, and performance. She received her MFA from School of Visual Arts. Her work has been shown nationally and internationally at such institutions as the Aldrich Contemporary Art Museum, Museum of Contemporary Art Cleveland, Whitney Museum of American Art, Brooklyn Museum, the Kitchen, Parasol Unit Foundation for Contemporary Art, and Museum of Contemporary Art (MCA) Chicago. She is a recipient of the Rome Prize from the American Academy in Rome and the Louis Comfort Tiffany Biennial Award. Her work is in the collections of the Museum of Modern Art in New York, Brooklyn Museum, Whitney Museum of American Art, and MCA Chicago, among others.

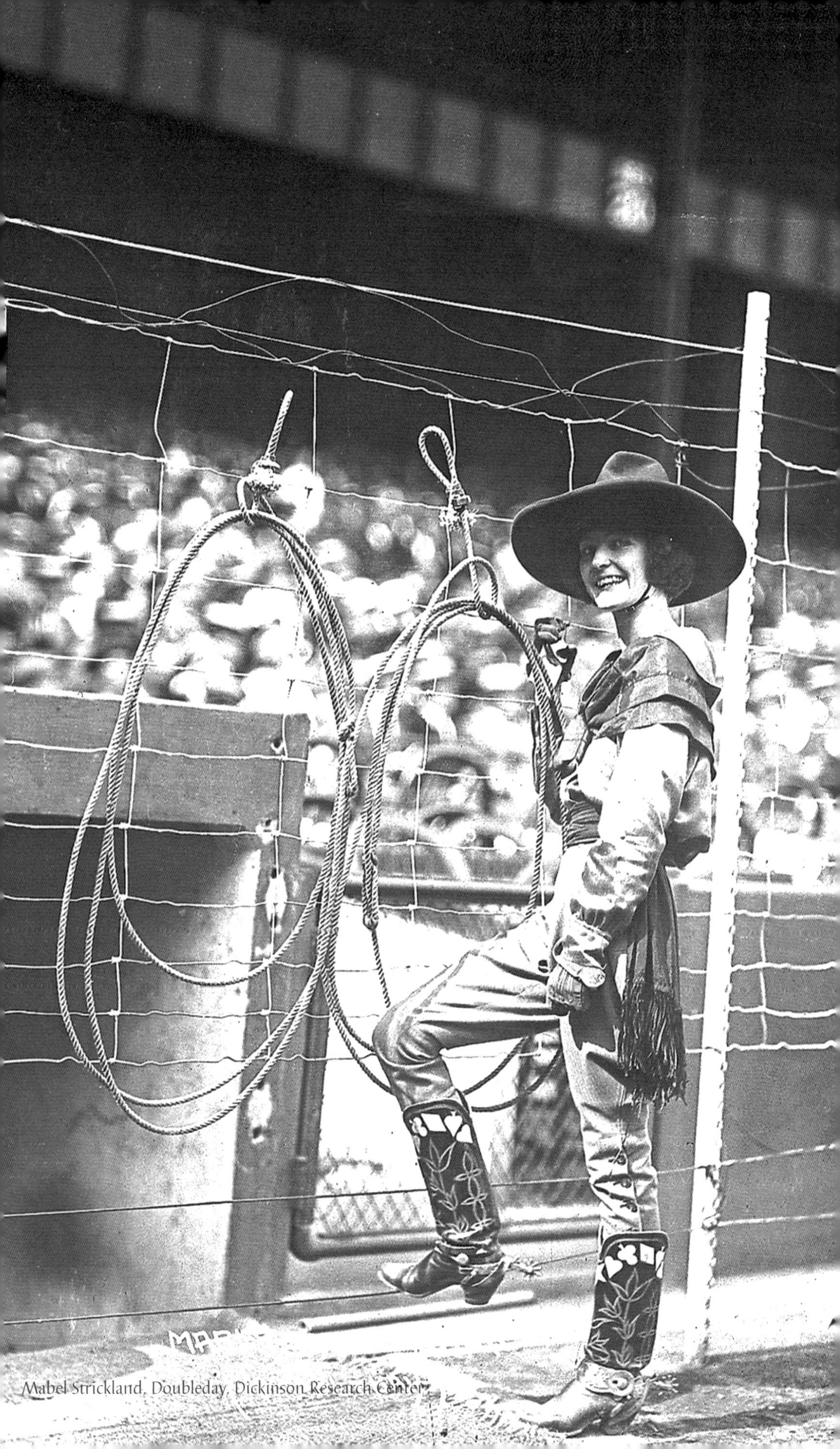

Mabel Strickland, Doubleday, Dickinson Research Center

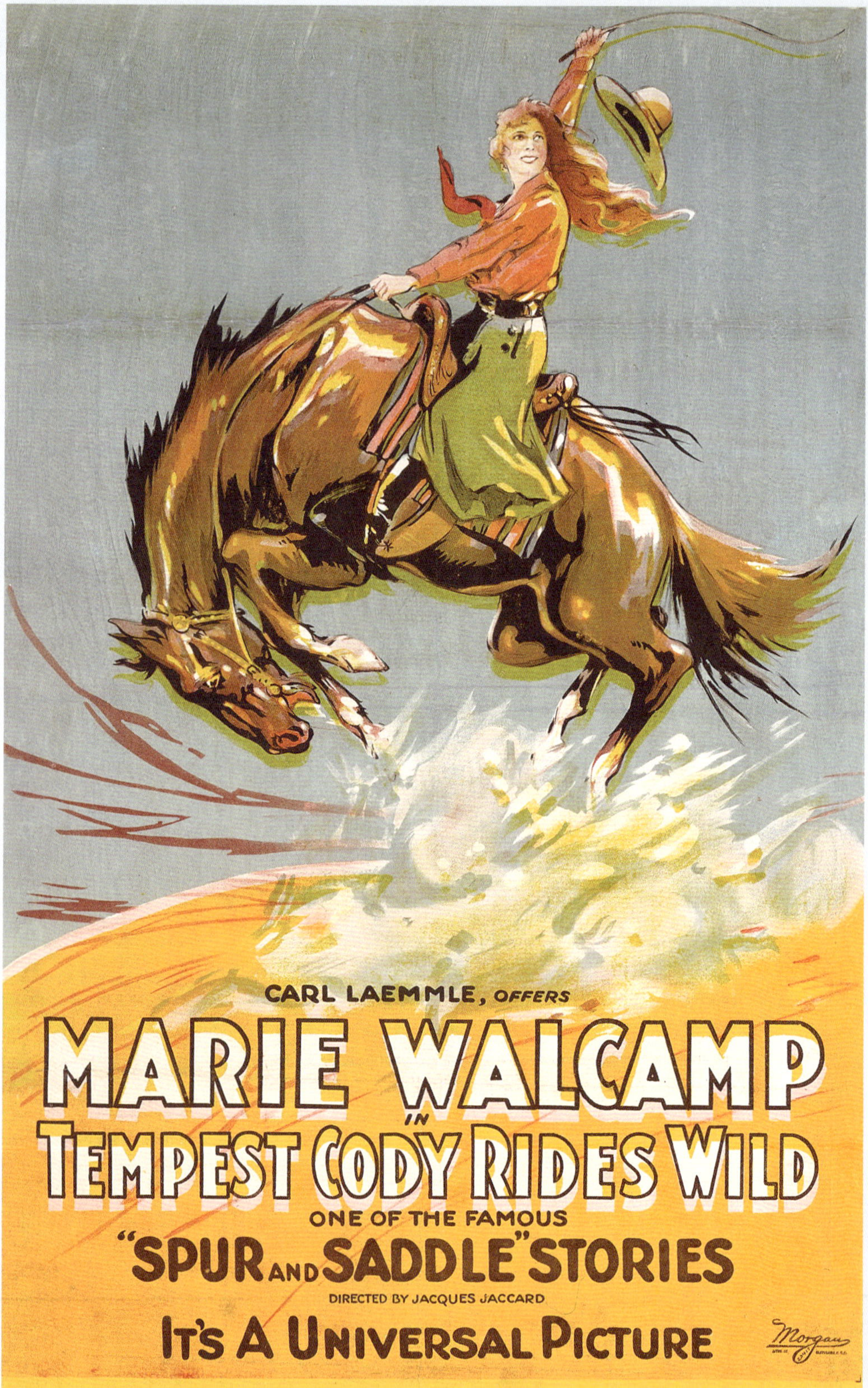

Marie Walcamp movie poster, 1919, Autry National Center

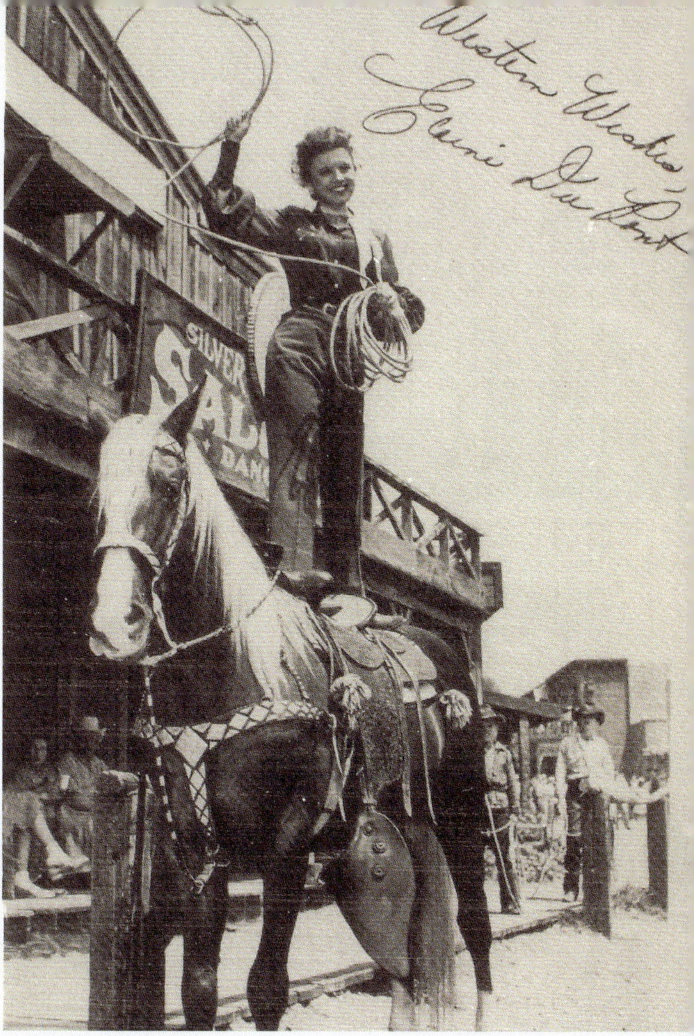

Elaine DuPont, 1939–1949,
Autry National Center

Blanche McGaughey, Pendleton Round-Up, Autry National Center

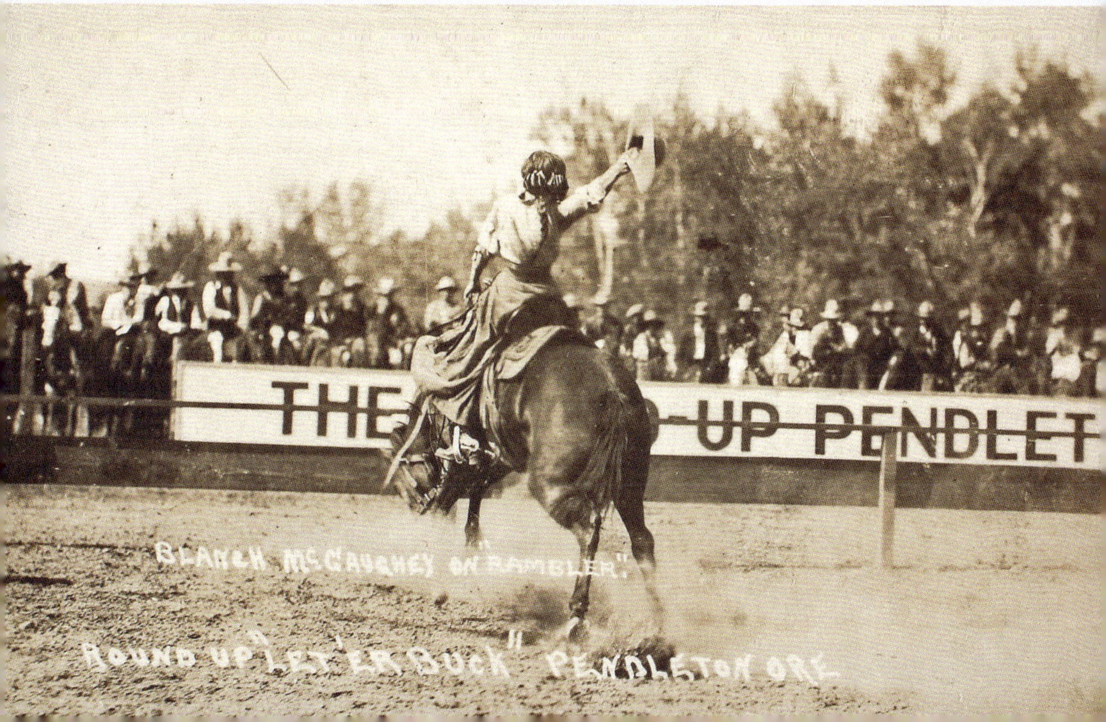

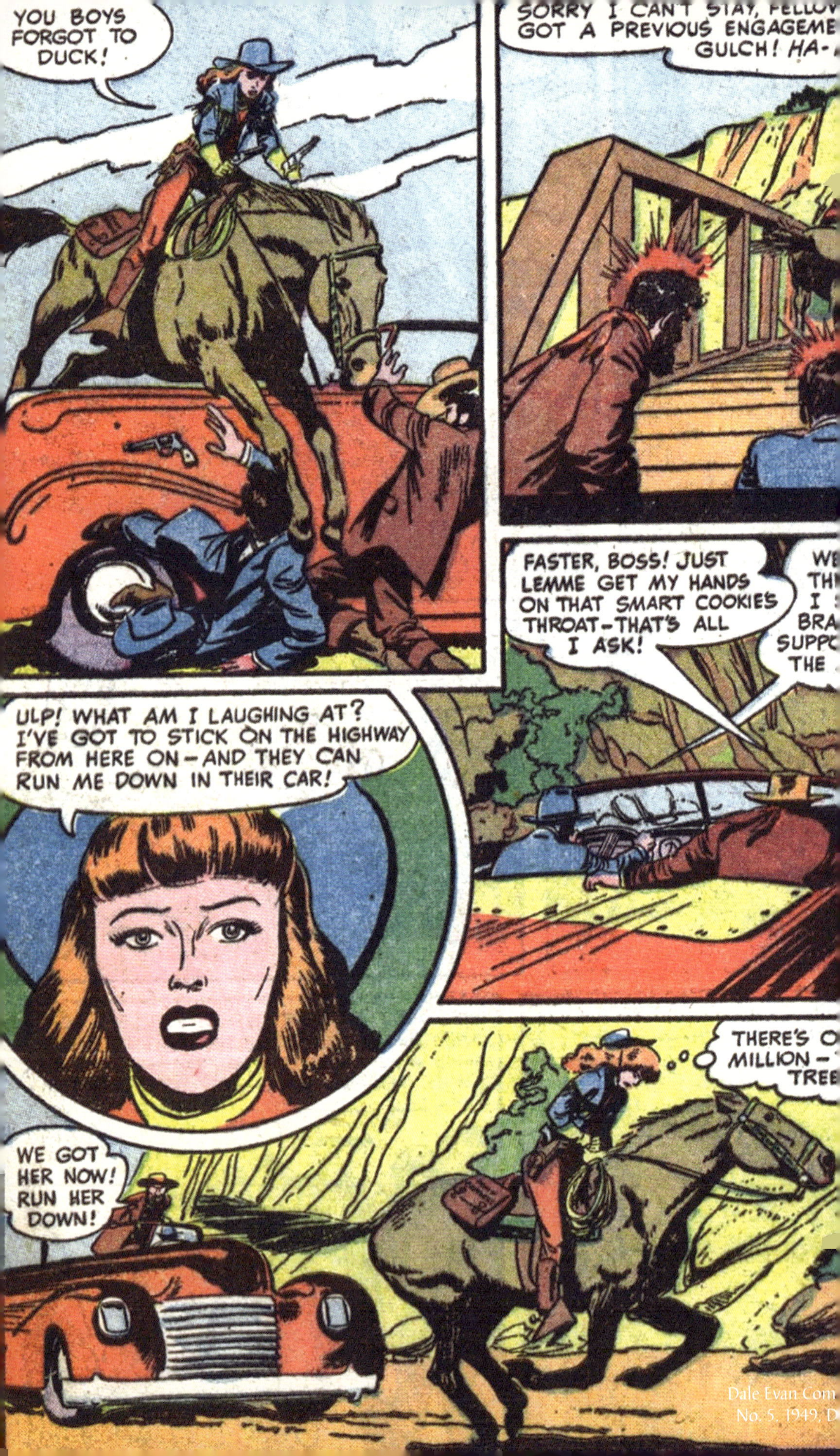

Dale Evan Com
No. 5, 1949, D

On the occasion of her first solo exhibition at Betty Cuningham Gallery, Dustup *(September 6–October 6, 2012), Nancy Davidson sat down with Kate Gilmore, an accomplished artist herself, to do an interview for the* Brooklyn Rail. *They discussed Davidson's sculpture and video, taking over spaces, bulbous parts, color, the Wild West, and unruly women. Their conversation, reprinted here, appeared in the September 2012 issue. Published monthly in Brooklyn, New York, the* Rail *is a journal of arts, culture, and politics, featuring interviews with artists, critics, and curators, as well as fiction, poetry, and coverage of music, dance, film, and theater.*

KATE GILMORE (*Brooklyn Rail*)**:** I thought talking about how I first fell in love with your work would be a good place to start. I've known your work for a long time, but I didn't really get a maximal experience of it until I saw "Double Exposure" in *Fantasy Underfoot*, the 47th Corcoran Biennial at the Corcoran [Gallery of Art] in Washington, D.C., in 2003. I walked in and saw this massive blowup structure taking over the entire architecture of the museum. I knew of the piece but you don't really know a piece until you see it in a place like that. I thought, "Badass—awesome!" It was an unapologetic female sculpture, and in such massive terms. I fell in love with the scale of the piece, the color of the piece, the sexuality of the piece, and the politics of the piece. I would particularly love to hear about the conversation between the sculpture and the space in which it was installed.

NANCY DAVIDSON: "Double Exposure" was commissioned specifically for the Beaux Arts atrium space in which Ronald Bladen had installed the giant X for the '67 exhibition *Scale as Content*. I had seen photographs of that exhibition and the curator, Jonathan Binstock suggested I consider making a work for that atrium. I immediately thought of putting a giant female form in that space, which would be both enormous in its scale and aggressive in its unruliness. It is enormous: 20 by 20 by 36 feet.

A red double-sphere form that can be viewed both from above and below, it was suspended by a blue rope in the middle of this elegant space, swaying gently, almost as if breathing. It gave me deep pleasure to see it in that space and think about the Ronald Bladen on one side of the atrium and Tony Smith on the other. From 1967 to 2003. In a little over 30 years you could have a piece that represents sculpture in all of its minimal-maximalness with content that was completely unacknowledged in the late '60s. I gained an understanding and perspective of the body as a primary form through feminism.

GILMORE: What's interesting is when I walked into the Corcoran I started to laugh. I laughed because it was funny, immediately funny, this kind of big red bulbous thing taking over this very traditional space. It went so against what we're supposed to see in that space. I laughed because I was uncomfortable and I could see that other people were uncomfortable. Humor is such a big part of the language of your work. Could you talk a little about this?

DAVIDSON: First of all, there is this transitory pleasure in looking at "Double Exposure." The work is engaged with spectatorship and the interaction, reaction, and attention to an implied social structure that sets up an often irrepressible release of laughter. You're complicit in this seduction: you laugh at the enormous breasts, the big butt, and suddenly it's like, "Oh my God, what am I laughing at, why is this sexual thing making me so uncomfortable?" There's a manipulation in this. There's also my own ambivalence: I embrace being a woman but also deal with the social structure of our culture and the various ways in which women are portrayed and expected to be. I'm interested in the subversive potential of humor. It catches you from behind: "What am I laughing at? Why am I finding this pleasurable? Is this offensive?"

GILMORE: But there's such darkness that underlies that humor.

DAVIDSON: Much humor is also involved with narrative. In the late '80s and the early '90s there was an increase in the popularity of female comedians. They discussed their own lives and experiences like male comedians did. There was an attitude of anything goes. Anything is possible with humor, so they didn't back away from transgressive or unruly aspects of their personalities. They were women using every aspect of their physical being and their interactions with people and putting it out there. There is a strength in using one's own experiences and body, particularly when taking on the role of the fool—not a traditional position for women. Contrary to laughing at women in, say, the '60s or '70s, the complicity of women laughing at women was not an acceptable thing to do without making women feel uncomfortable or humiliated about what was being laughed at.

GILMORE: So, are women laughing at *your* women?

DAVIDSON: Yes, I see women laughing at the hybrid bodies that I've constructed. It's a knowing laughter enjoyed through sexuality, humor, aggressiveness, and excess. That excess is a polymorphous humor that just spreads. Body humor is about women, about men, about babies, animals. If you enjoy it you have to know that you're implicated. Laughter is uncontrollable and unruly.

GILMORE: You talk about the unruly female quite a bit. Could you talk about how this becomes a social critique?

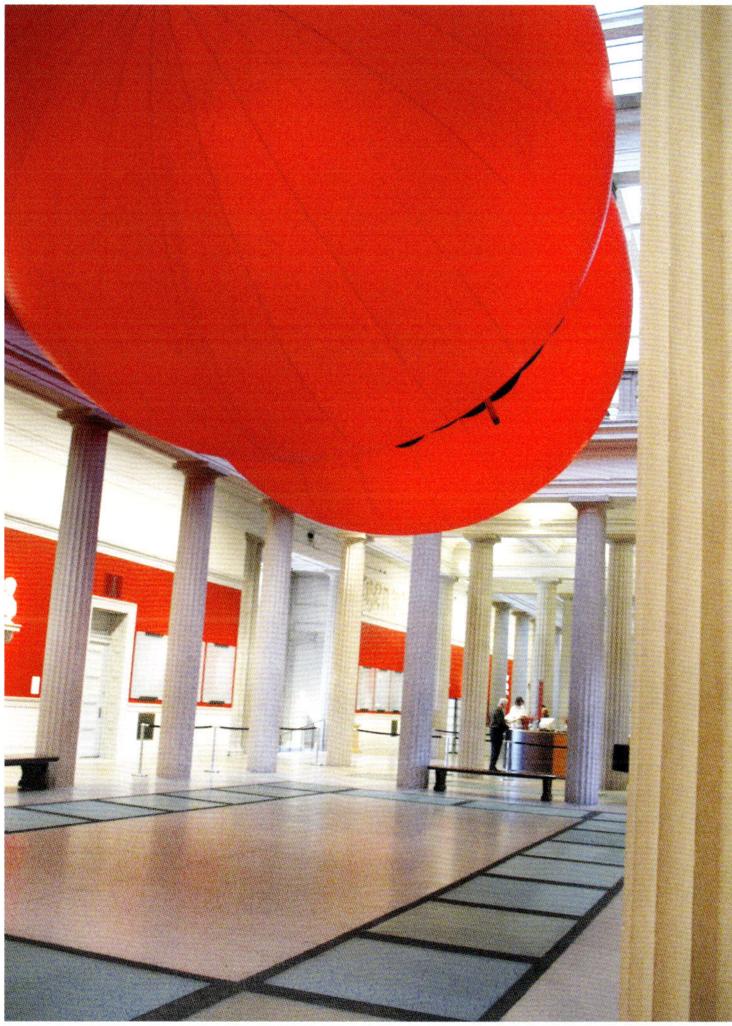

"Double Exposure," 2002/3. Corcoran commission. 20' x 20' x34'. Vinyl-coated nylon, light, fabric, and foam. Courtesy the artist.

DAVIDSON: Yes, it's related to how I also use the word carnivalesque, which I understand as a state of social critique. Sometimes it prescribes a space where all kinds of things can happen. Festivals in the late Middle Ages saw inversions of authority: men dressing up as women, women dressing up as men, people mooning each other. Mikhail Bakhtin coined the term carnivalesque to describe a mode in which assumptions about power are reversed. There are vestigial aspects of this today in celebrations of Halloween, Carnival, demonstrations, and parades. In Carnivals in Germany and Switzerland you will see people wearing big masks, animal/people heads, hybrid bodies, a baker's hat with horns on a cow's head. That kind of play is the open space for critique outside of social order. I believe contemporary art carries some of the task of the unruly social space. My work can be thought of as a kind of play, sculpture, overblown, formal, with references to material and popular culture.

GILMORE: Let's talk a bit more about how popular culture comes into play in your work.

DAVIDSON: Growing up in the '50s I was very much aware of popular figures like Elvis Presley and Marilyn Monroe. When I work with one of these popular figures as an inspiration, media, visual attributes, and poses transform a person like Mae West into a trope. In my piece ["Maebe"] I am trading on the audience's knowledge of Mae West to some extent, so that the work steps forward toward the audience with its back-loaded references. I want my work to make a comment. I want it to be desirable. I want my work to be a part of the active social space of spectacle.

What is the meaning of signs in our contemporary culture? Why use a particular kind of fabric that stretches tight over an inflatable that looks like flesh? These are immediate signifiers to people: "Oh, I know what that means!" So then they step forward a little bit more. They open up to the pleasures of the unstable meaning. It's both a social critique and celebration. I'm not separate from this culture; I'm not separate from the pleasures that I put out there and make fun of, make light of, or play with. That's all part of who I am as well as where I am.

GILMORE: It's interesting that you talk about how you want things to be desirable, but you also want to go against that. Many people reference the grotesque when discussing your work. I would be interested to hear you talk about the relationship between the desire to be desired and the grotesque.

DAVIDSON: One time when I was making a piece, I put something on it and something else fell off of it. I looked at it and thought, "It looks like it's a striptease. It's losing its clothes or something." Then I thought, "Oh, oh, wait a minute."

When immersed in a topsy-turvy perspective, desire and repulsion often become intertwined. Just as air-brushed beauty can become grotesque, a certain beauty can often be noticed and appreciated in the grotesque. That's the transgressive aspect of the work, the attempt to present visual aspects of these extremes simultaneously.

GILMORE: I do think of the Corcoran piece as a kind of stripper. I mean, she's hanging out there for people to see, and people can just, like, put some dollars in her ropes.

DAVIDSON: I've seen children just run screaming, playing underneath that piece. Children are so directly attached to play and to their physical relationship to objects. I wanted that piece to be undeniable in its physicality.

GILMORE: I think we should talk about color and materials as this holds so much content in your work.

DAVIDSON: Eva Hesse's work is important to me now and always. Her materials were so unlike other artists' of her time. She used soft materials related to aspects of the body. There are great photographs of her holding some of her sculptures. It looks like she had a relationship with them, a tenderness to them that I had not seen in other photos of artists and their work. She used materials like rubber, latex, and nets, and she used systems that started out as a grid and ended in chaos. In the early '70s I was very much taken with the implications of her work. At the time my work was black-and-white. After working for four years in black and white, I decided that I wanted to work with color. The work was still very abstract, but one day I picked up colored paint sticks and it changed the forms of my work. I began looking at Balinese dance and movement. Fast forward to 1992. I had an idea about weather balloons. I wanted to take up a good deal of space with a material that was lightweight, so I could move the work around myself. That's something about my work; it's always been big. I sent for a weather balloon. It was about five feet in diameter. Every one of my pieces begins as a sphere. They're latex, and they have this great nozzle where you put the air in. I blew it up, took a rope, and tied it off at the neck. I squeezed it into a clothing rack, so the clothing rack held it in the middle and it just hung there. I looked at it and I thought, "This is really funny. This is really nasty. This is really sexy. This is a body; this is flesh; this is enormous, I want to make work like this." And that's where my work with inflatables started. When I researched the balloons, I realized I could get them in colors. I used the color as a way to draw attention to the work, to make it more noticeable.

GILMORE: Why do you want to be noticed? Why do you want to take over an entire space?

DAVIDSON: I think that really has to do with occupying a space that had been occupied differently. Early on I was interested in Donald Judd's stack pieces and his use of auto-body materials and colors. I have been interested in serial, multiple forms that create a structure, and the minimal sculptures that took up an enormous amount of space. So I wanted to be part of that dialogue, with sculpture that is both enormous and materially very lightweight. There's more to it than its weight because my large pieces are often filled with air. There is a considerable dialogue around the weightiness of sculpture, its seriousness and its structural integrity. I see my work as part of that dialogue. Being part of a serious dialogue by adding humor challenges the status quo and pomposity.

GILMORE: Can we talk a little more about the deadly seriousness?

DAVIDSON: I want to call the attention of the viewer to the possibilities of a social order where the pleasures and playfulness and sexuality of women is respected and admired. I don't want it to be thought of as a utopian——

GILMORE: No, it's not utopian.

DAVIDSON: Yeah. [*Laughs.*] I want my work acknowledged as taking a critical position, at the same time being completely playful and pleasurable.

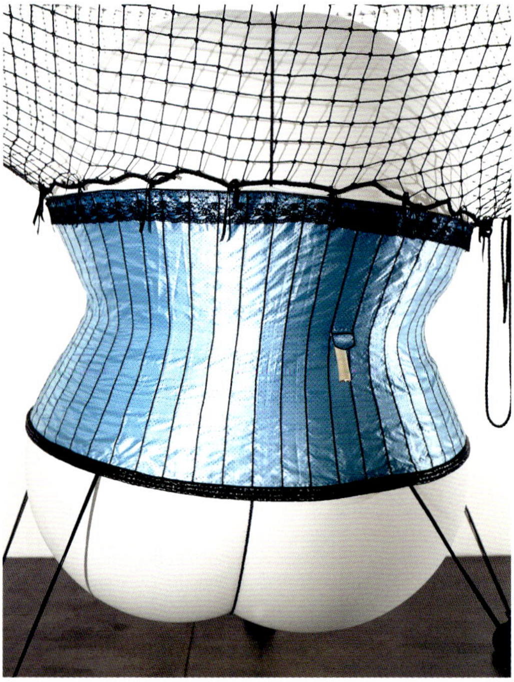

"Maebe," 1997. Installation view. 96" × 60" × 60". Latex, fabric, net, plaster, and rope. Courtesy the artist.

GILMORE: That's a very stereotypical female condition.

DAVIDSON: What about Jeff Koons?

GILMORE: Right, no, that's true, that's true.

DAVIDSON: What about Mike Kelly who wanted to play with children's things, and at the same time take a very critical position? I'm saying the difference is that I'm proposing a criticality in the face of celebration. I'm proposing difference as a way of celebrating a more open and human structure without privileging dominance by one gender or the other.

GILMORE: Dominance can be a larger conversation too. Those who are on the in, and those who are on the out, right?

DAVIDSON: I think it's more than that. I think it can take a position that moves out into the world. Can it go out in a park? Can it go to a festival? Can it move around? Can people understand it? Do people have to be knowledgeable about abstraction to understand it? Maybe not. Not if it addresses concerns in the world that step outside a certain art world structure and starts to address issues that are beyond that. I want to do that with "Dustup." As a child in the '50s, I was inspired by the cowgirl and her can-do spirit. When researching the cowgirl with a grant from Creative Capital, I realized as a child I had been taken in by this characterization of a cowgirl. It was important to me because it presented a woman who was outside of the cultural structure. She was unruly, she was beyond the rules. When I went out west and started looking at rodeos, I realized that the rodeo cowgirl maintained her own place outside the structure of society. She did things that were unacceptable. That character, that trope, was fascinating to me because it worked with all of the ideas I had about popular characters, tropes, and stereotypes, but a very real American icon, a Western icon. There are aspects of it that are very inspirational and make people want to do things and create things in their lives. That's the kind of transgressive complexity, self-motivated dominance I'm attracted to in popular culture.

GILMORE: When I look at this new body of work at Betty's, I think about *Annie Get Your Gun*. You know [*sings*], "Anything you can do, I can do better." For those who aren't Broadway-crazy like myself, it's about a girl who's trying to do everything that this boy is doing. That is, on a larger scale, the conversation behind much of the work that you make. You participate within your own terms, but also take the rules that exist and force your own systems onto them. This cowgirl, this *Annie Get Your Gun* character, enters this beautiful Chelsea gallery.

You're more known for sculpture and these inflatables, but you've also been making videos for the past few years, and there will be a video in the show. I think we should talk about that transition, how has video entered your life.

DAVIDSON: Right. Well, my first work with video was in 1999. I'd been looking at the inflatables in my studio, how they blow up and they look wonderful and full, and then they lose air and deflate.

GILMORE: They perform.

DAVIDSON: They do perform, and then they die, or they become this shriveled thing on the floor. It's not something you see in my work because when I do the pieces, they're always fully inflated, they're at their most bulbous selves and when they start deflating then they have to be quickly inflated again.

The first video I made in '99 was called "Breathless." The subject was a pink balloon. It blew up and it deflated and it bounced around. I worked with a filmmaker, Ken Kobland, and sound artist Judith Dunbar. She had recorded sounds of balloons inflating and deflating, making really squeaky sounds. I was fascinated with the fixing of time and editing. After that I bought a little video camera and it accompanied me when I went places. I did a short video of the Corcoran piece in '03. Then in '05 when I was out west doing research at the Cowgirl Hall of Fame and Museum in Fort Worth, the women working there said to me, "You should go next door and see the Women's Professional Rodeo." I've never been to a rodeo and I didn't know what to expect. The next day I went and saw a woman named Jan Youren. It was her last ride after 47 years of riding bucking broncos. I had my camera with me so I captured her doing this ride; it was fascinating to me on many levels. I couldn't believe someone who was [63] years old would be riding and falling because you always fall off the horse at the rodeo. It became an obsession for me. I had to find out who were these rodeo cowgirls, what was their history. I started traveling to all kinds of rodeos, both men and women and I found out many things about rodeo. The rodeos for the women were in poorly-lit spaces and the money that they won was a fraction of what the male rodeo-riders won. After a year and a half of videotaping different rodeos I began working on a video. I was fascinated with the space of the rodeo, the rink, the ritual, and reenactment. When I reviewed the clips I found the men's bull riding of more interest to me visually. The bulls were more outrageous, the arena had better lighting. The videos of the women riders were almost unusable due to the poor lighting in the arenas they performed in. I began to make "All Stories Are True," the video in the current show. It's about the eight-second ride. Every rider comes out, spins around, holds on for as long as he can, and then flies off. If he's lucky not to get trampled by the bull, he runs off and comes back for the next ride. Their ritual reminded me of the myth of Icarus. I cut the video very tightly to just have these aspects of the ride, the spinning, the flying, the falling in repetition. I think about it as extreme gender display. My show has both the inflatable "cowgirl sculptures" suspended in a dust ball dustup, and a video of male cowboys in another room.

GILMORE: When I was watching the video, I was really taken with the flashbulbs. How do you see that aspect of the video in relation to the show and to the sculpture, but also in relation to the way you've been dealing with pop culture in your other works?

DAVIDSON: When I looked at the tapes, there were many light flashes, because people were photographing the riders. Rodeo is an extreme spectacle and every aspect is part of its ritual. The sound content is as important as the visuals. It begins with a droning sound and the flashbulb sounds, then slowly the noise of the crowd and the AM-radio hard rock takes over. It represents the way we look at athletes and physical prowess and a kind of idealism that's anything but ideal. I was completely unfamiliar with rodeo yet within that space all the tropes that I've ever thought about in relationship to popular culture are there. Video provides a time-space dimension that sculpture delivers in a different way. After finishing "All Stories Are True," I made a short piece using the cowgirl sculptures as puppets. It's titled "I've

Been Everywhere." It is a video about cowgirl puppets coming to life. I think about my pieces as if they were strange beings, these playful, destructive, childlike beings. "Dustup" was inspired by classic comic dustball images, an epic battle, all tossed up together in the air, legs everywhere, bulbous form everywhere, leather hanging everywhere.

GILMORE: Leather? [*Laughs.*]

DAVIDSON: Yes, there's leather and it is a true story.

Acknowledgments

My gratitude to the John Simon Guggenheim Memorial Foundation for its support, along with special thanks to Ruby Lerner and Sean Elwood at Creative Capital, whose enthusiasm inspired me from the start of my cowgirl project. Betty Cuningham's foresight and vision saw the work through to the first exhibition of the *Dustup* project, and Kathy Goncharov and the staff at the Boca Raton Museum of Art did a superb job installing an expanded exhibition of my cowgirl work. In forming my project into a book, I must extend special thanks to Riley Hooker and Megan Feehan for their innovative design concept; Jessica Brier, Renée Laegreid, and Leisl Carr Childers for their essays; Kate Gilmore and Phong Bui at the *Brooklyn Rail* for their interview and publication; and Gideon Barnett for his brilliant photographs. Research for the book and the sculpture that preceded it was made possible with the generous assistance of Marva Felchlin, director, Libraries and Archives of the Autry National Center. Throughout, I depended on the support of Greg Drasler.

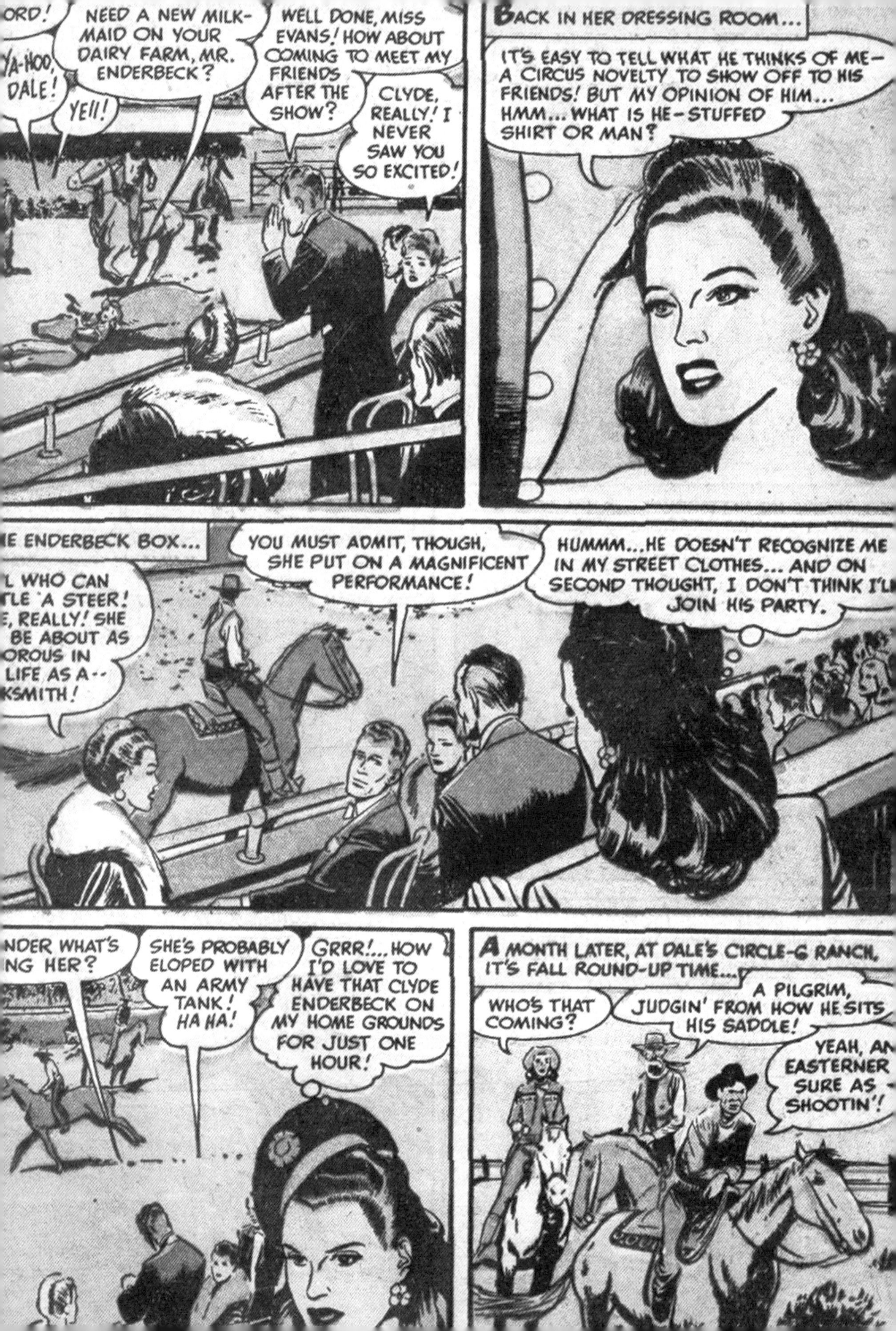
ORD!
YA-HOO, DALE!
YEll!
NEED A NEW MILK-MAID ON YOUR DAIRY FARM, MR. ENDERBECK?
WELL DONE, MISS EVANS! HOW ABOUT COMING TO MEET MY FRIENDS AFTER THE SHOW?
CLYDE, REALLY! I NEVER SAW YOU SO EXCITED!
BACK IN HER DRESSING ROOM...
IT'S EASY TO TELL WHAT HE THINKS OF ME— A CIRCUS NOVELTY TO SHOW OFF TO HIS FRIENDS! BUT MY OPINION OF HIM... HMM... WHAT IS HE—STUFFED SHIRT OR MAN?
HE ENDERBECK BOX...
L WHO CAN TLE A STEER! E, REALLY! SHE BE ABOUT AS OROUS IN LIFE AS A-- KSMITH!
YOU MUST ADMIT, THOUGH, SHE PUT ON A MAGNIFICENT PERFORMANCE!
HUMMM...HE DOESN'T RECOGNIZE ME IN MY STREET CLOTHES... AND ON SECOND THOUGHT, I DON'T THINK I'L JOIN HIS PARTY.
NDER WHAT'S NG HER?
SHE'S PROBABLY ELOPED WITH AN ARMY TANK! HA HA!
GRRR!... HOW I'D LOVE TO HAVE THAT CLYDE ENDERBECK ON MY HOME GROUNDS FOR JUST ONE HOUR!
A MONTH LATER, AT DALE'S CIRCLE-G RANCH, IT'S FALL ROUND-UP TIME...
WHO'S THAT COMING?
A PILGRIM, JUDGIN' FROM HOW HE SITS HIS SADDLE!
YEAH, AN EASTERNER SURE AS SHOOTIN'!